FRAMES OF MIND

FRAMES OF MIND

Constraints on the Common-Sense
Conception of the Mental

BY
ADAM MORTON

CLARENDON PRESS · OXFORD
1980

Oxford University Press, Walton Street, Oxford OX2 6DP

OXFORD LONDON GLASGOW
NEW YORK TORONTO MELBOURNE WELLINGTON
KUALA LUMPUR SINGAPORE JAKARTA HONG KONG TOKYO
DELHI BOMBAY CALCUTTA MADRAS KARACHI
NAIROBI DAR ES SALAAM CAPE TOWN

© *Adam Morton 1980*

Published in the United States by
Oxford University Press, New York

British Library Cataloguing in Publication Data

Morton, Adam
  Frames of mind.
  1. Social perception
  I. Title
153.7′5   HM 132   79-41315

ISBN 0-19-824607-2

*Printed and bound in Great Britain by
Morrison & Gibb Ltd, London and Edinburgh*

CONTENTS

LIST OF DIAGRAMS

INTRODUCTION

Our understanding of one another, and of ourselves, results from a bargain with ignorance. We are ignorant of most of the deeper causes of our actions, and of the laws that govern the workings of our minds. And yet we often succeed in understanding and explaining actions, thought, emotions. We manage this in two ways: by exploiting the fact that we, the understanders and explainers, are people, and work along roughly the same lines as those we understand and explain, and by using our psychological vocabulary, our stock of terms that describe the mental and explain what we do, in a somewhat peculiar way, so that the import of what one says on a particular occasion gets adjusted to fit the facts of that occasion.

Or so I claim. The aim of the book is to work out two more specific ideas, on the border of psychology and philosophy. One is a new version of an old picture of how people understand each other. I think that one often knows why someone did something because one can imagine what it was like for that person. But this imagining is not what it has often been taken to be. The other concerns common-sense psychology, the lore about people that packages our common concepts of belief, memory, desire, intention, and so on. I think that it consists neither of a fixed body of empirical principles, like a rough-and-ready scientific theory, nor of a fixed understanding of the content of these concepts, like a rather chatty collection of dictionary entries. Rather, as I explain in Chapter I, it consists in a constancy underlying innumerable improvisations and variations in the principles we apply and the concepts we use. One learns what methods and principles to use not by extracting them from a store of accepted doctrine but by using one's acquaintance with the varied stream of explanations and attributions to project another explanation or attribution, that is stylistically coherent with what others and oneself have done before. It is like composing within a musical tradition, or giving a legal judgement in accordance with a body of precedents, or speaking a dialect of a language. (The last of these seems particularly close.) One's ability to make the projection is partly a matter of seeing patterns and generalizing, and partly of using certain innate and rather specific capacities.

These two ideas need not, on the face of it, have much to do with each other. Their connection lies in the particular way in which I develop each. The same themes keep coming up, in particular those expressed in my first paragraph. What it all amounts to is that I don't think that we have a set of beliefs which delimit what we can regard as having a mind. We do not say: minds are anything that satisfy these conditions. Rather, we say: minds are anything we can understand by using these capacities. 'These capacities', and the constraints they put on our conception of the mental, are the subject of the book.

If I am right, then the common-sense conception of mind cannot be analysed in purely common-sense terms. If there were a simple set of assertions or conditions which constituted the content of the concept then we would have a typical philosopher's task of stating them as explicitly and usefully as possible. It would not be easy, but one could do it by being a sufficiently reflective subscriber to common sense. If there is no such set of assertions or conditions, though, then the job looks different. Some real psychological conjectures may have to be risked, in trying to describe the capacities that people bring to metal attribution and explanation. Armchair psychology may do as well as the real laboratory product for part of what is needed, but there is always the danger that more facts or a better theory will come along to refute one. And some terms may have to be invented, to capture regularities in everyday talk of minds that are not evident from the terms in which they are usually expressed.[1]

---

[1] I shall acknowledge particular debts as they occur. I must express a more general gratitude to Paul Benacerraf and C. G. Hempel for having taught me some philosophy, to Fabrizio Mondadori, Amelie Oksenberg Rorty, and David Rosenthal for helping me think I had something to say, to Andrew Woodfield for an extremely useful set of comments on an earlier draft, and to the University of Ottawa for providing me with a home.

I

COMMON-SENSE PSYCHOLOGY

THE AUTHORITY OF A CULTURE

Nothing is more characteristic of everyday human life than the innumerable ordinary answers, giving the reasons for people's actions and the states of their minds. So innumerable and so ordinary are they, that we often overlook the questions they are answers to. It is when the answers do not appear with their usual ease that the questions appear, and we explicitly ask 'Why are you quarrelling with her?', 'What is his opinion of you?' Then, finding the answers often takes all our intelligence and sophistication. Practically the whole culture and practically all of our capacities to use it can come to a focus here, in explaining action and describing states of mind. The more the sophistication that is or has to be brought to bear on the difficult cases, the more the answers vary. Depending on what one believes or expects, in what ways one is civilized, or what one's attitude to the people in question is, one will find different motives behind their actions, and use them to make different explanations of what they do. And then tracing back the origins of these disagreements to the simpler, apparently more unproblematic, cases, one finds that quite parallel disagreements are possible there too.

The aim of this book is to elaborate this assimilation of the easy cases to the hard ones, to describe skills and beliefs, parts of inherited nature and acquired sophistication, that make a unity of what I will call common-sense psychology, that is, of the complex of skills and beliefs that we bring to bear on explanations of action and attributions of states of mind. The eventual drift of my argument is that there is a sense in which the opposite assimilation, of sophisticated ascriptions and explanations to naïve ones, is as revealing. That is, that sophisticated, culture-coloured, explaining and ascribing have as much of the lack of freedom, the pre-formedness, that marks the naïve or immediate way of doing these things, as the naïve has of the dependence on the details of a culture that marks the sophisticated. But that conclusion cannot even be properly formulated until we have found a satisfactory way of stating the prior idea that there is a unity to the psychological, that quick intuitive ascriptions and deliberate sophisticated explanations are parts of a single system of practice and belief.

THEORIES

There certainly is a body of beliefs which people in a given culture at a given time bring to explaining and understanding one another. And some properties of this body of belief are clearly like those of some other organized bits of doctrine, such as scientific theories. Other resemblances between this lore and formal theories are less clear, but can be argued for in interesting ways. The attractions of likening common-sense psychology to an informal version of a scientific theory can become very striking. There are three important resemblances between explicit theories and the kind of lore in question. First, and fairly uncontroversially, both involve a body of assertions which with practice one can use to explain various things, under some circumstances predict other things, and which do this in part because they possess a certain homogeneity. Then, more disputably, both may be taken to make definite claims, which aim for truth and which when they fail are usually false, about particular determinate subject-matters. More controversially yet, both may be taken as consisting of conjectures about the best explanations of various phenomena, explanations which while often well established owe their acceptance to the fact that better explanations or refuting evidence have not turned up.

I believe that all three of these resemblances between explicit theories and common-sense psychology do hold. I think that the last two, the controversial ones, are connected with equally basic differences. And I think that if we are explicit enough about what we intend by 'theory' and what alternative is being suggested, these differences are enough to show that common-sense psychology is not a theory but something subtly different, what I shall call a scheme. I must begin with the resemblances, though.

A theory, to speak somewhat prescriptively, is a body of assertions whose terms refer to individuals and properties, and which is transmitted and evolves in accordance with the intention that it assert the truth about them. A theory need not be stated or statable by any single person. It need not be precise. Nor need everyone who subscribes to it know quite what his subscription commits him to. But one must use the theory as if those one had obtained it from intended its terms to refer to objective realities, and the changes one makes in the theory, by removing existing beliefs or adding new ones, must be made with the intention of increasing the proportion of true to false assertions about those realities. These two requirements are related. For when evidence leads one to believe that objects O have property P, then disagreement with a theory that asserts 'O's don't have P' only makes sense on the assumption that the intent of the theory is to refer to O's, the same O's the evidence is about. (Otherwise, one would just say: there is an alternative theory, and it supposes some things it calls O's, and it supposes them not to have P; *my* theory supposes O's that have P.) And, the other way around, if one's understanding of a theory and of the terms in it, is that it is intended to be about certain particular objects and properties, then one's interpretation of evidence, or of the consequences of other theories, as indicating facts about *those* objects, will force one to expand, modify, or deny the original theory.[1]

What subscribers to a theory have in common, then, is first that they share a common conception of what the theory is

---

[1] These formulations, and a lot of what follows, are a digest of current ideas in the philosophy of science. It seems to me that the characteristic picture of science found in the work of C. G. Hempel, see the essays in *Aspects of Scientific Explanation* (Macmillan, New York, 1965), is in its emphasis on the autonomy of theory, part of the later development that leads for example to Hilary Putnam's 'What Theories are Not', *Philosophical Papers*, vol. i (C.U.P., 1975), and 'Meaning and Reference', *Journal of Philosophy* 70, 1973, pp. 699–711, and to Hartry Field's 'Theory Change and the Indeterminacy of Reference', *Journal of Philosophy* 70, 1973, pp. 462–81.

about. This is a matter mostly of their grasp of the theory's terms. It may take the form of a set of beliefs about what kind of thing the terms denote (e.g. the descriptions of molecules learned in school chemistry), what their typical causes and effects are, and what forms these causal connections take (e.g. how laboratory phenomena are typically related to chemical reactions). Then the actual facts about the causes and effects in the area in question determine exactly what the referents of the terms are. (For example, they determine that 'molecule' applies to certain congeries of atoms, and not others, and that 'valence' applies to the willingness to wander of the electrons in an atom's outer layer or two.) When one understands the terms, one can understand what the theory says about them. One needs explicit knowledge of only a few of the theory's assertions. For one knows how to get more from other people. As long as one can tell when another's use of a term is intended to refer to the same things as one's use of that or another term, one can use others— particularly the experts, authorities, teachers—as repositories of assertions one cannot produce for oneself. The result is that by acquiring a fairly small number of beliefs one gets in touch with a large number of (putative) facts about things. In this way the characteristic semantic feature of terms in theories, that they refer to objects causally related to various phenomena, in relative independence of what the theory says about them, serves a communicative purpose. It allows a theory to be the work and property of many people, where no one has to understand or do everything.

Not any collection of beliefs forms a theory. The unity of a theory, the way its terms rest semantically on one another and its assertions can be spread over a group of people, is something that most sets of assertions cannot have. Number all the commonly held beliefs, and take the 'theory' consisting of the prime numbered ones. There are no experts, no texts or techniques, no ways of generating it. It *couldn't* evolve as a unit or be criticized as one.

There are theories outside science too. There are bodies of belief which are capable of being held in co-operation by numbers of people, and which evolve as unities, by virtue of a shared understanding of how their terms refer to a determinate set of objects and properties. For example, the common-sense theory of which activities are healthy or unhealthy, or the theory that hard work and obedience in childhood develops a sensible and industrious adult. Or consider astrology or the doctrine of original sin. And then there are non-scientific imitations of scientific theories. The theory that the actions of entrepreneurs acting competitively in the market will result in a fair and satisfactory distribution of goods and positions, seems to be held by many people in a way that while definitely theory-like does not amount to any similar theories of economics or social science. I find it interesting that all the examples that occur to one here are faintly disreputable. There is a reason for this. Science is the best way of running a theory; we build into it whatever we find to be a good theory-managing technique. So any body of beliefs that is not a part of science will be either a poor imitation of a scientific theory or something that is not a theory at all, for example a scheme.

THE THEORY THEORY

We all draw on a stock of beliefs—and conjectures and suggestions—about how people are likely to act and react and what the reasons for various actions are likely to be. Life would be impossible if we couldn't. These beliefs clearly change through time and across cultures; one knows something essential about an age and a culture when one knows how actions are explained in it. The suggestion is that this stock of beliefs takes the form of a theory. If so, one wants to know how the theory is accessible —how one learns what its terms denote and how one gets in touch with those of its assertions one has not learned—and how it evolves—what evidence, what theoretical considerations, shake and change it.

Some of these questions have straightforward answers, at least in outline. There are 'experts' who transmit and evolve the 'theory'. They are novelists, moralists, and metaphysicians, among others; presumably the development and dissemination of ideas about how people work is one of the great social functions of literature. The learning of the theory must begin with the socialization of each individual, when very early in life each child begins to understand that there are other independent minds about him. The evidence: well, it may be as varied as the evidence affecting any theory is; one would suppose that it consists largely of increasingly telling estimates of the frequency with which rough generalizations about actions and motives hold. That is, most common-sense psychological principles take the form 'people often (sometimes almost always) act (reason, feel) as follows . . .'; with increasing experience one may expect to be able to see more justly what the import of the qualifiers 'often', 'sometimes', 'almost always' is. Then one can suggest which generalizations are likely to be illuminating, and one can suggest strategies for using them in uncovering motives and anticipating actions.

Ideas along these lines are very appealing to both philosophers and psychologists, now that in both subjects we are trying to construct realistic accounts of how we acquire our knowledge of each other's motives, beliefs, and the like. A large amount of recent work in the philosophy of mind and in social psychology can be taken as attempting to show what the concepts and typical principles of the theory would be, and how they could be understood. It is remarkable how the two approaches converge. In philosophy, the attractiveness of the theory theory is a result of disenchantment with both Cartesian and behaviouristic analyses of the concept of the mental. Once one begins to think of both of these as presenting cripplingly oversimplified pictures of what we are doing in ascribing states of mind to people, one can come to think of them as strangely similar in their limitations. Each takes as central an uncomplicated capacity to make observations: reflection, introspection, on the Cartesian account, the observation of behaviour on the behaviourist account. Each then takes the ascription of states of mind to oneself and others from this observational basis to require just induction and the definition of terms. The meanings of psychological words seem quite unproblematic, they can be given by any definitions that sum up the observations, of self or of behaviour, that would establish a term's application. There is no need for experts, no need for the body of beliefs about mind to have any unity beyond the coherence of each particular attribution.

It is natural, then, when one begins to see through these rhetorical screens to the real messiness of the concept of mind, whether it is from reading Strawson or Putnam[2] or from a fruitful confusion of psychological and philosophical considerations, that one should tend towards views whose positive consequences emphasize the dependence of particular ascriptions on something, a skill or a shared irreducible concept or a theory, that gets in the way of direct inferences from experience or behaviour to states of mind. Our grasp of what this something must be has got steadily more definitite over the past twenty years. It began with no more definite an idea than that it involved some sorts of socially instilled skills.

These skills clearly exist. Recent writers have described something like a step by step process by which they could be acquired. In the first place one learns the patterns of behaviour that are standard signs of various kinds of mental states. One need learn no definitions in the process; one just becomes capable of saying when these states are present. And then one learns, by a sort of conditioning, how to report of oneself that one is in one of these states. This second element is, too, based ultimately on one's behaviour, since it is because of what one does that others do whatever it is they do to condition one's readiness to avow one's state. Lastly, one learns to put these two together, and ascribe states, to oneself on the basis of one's behaviour as well as because of one's inclinations to avow, to others on the basis of their avowals, and various complicated combinations of these.

True as this all seems to be, it also seems to leave something out. These skills are not just picked up one by one because they are useful and because human nature is malleable. Their acquisition is a unity; one learns them all together, and in the process comes to understand something. One sign of this is their connection with socially instilled normative ideals, pictures of how one is to act if one is to be understood. We all know that we do not often actually fit into the details of the stereotypes of reasonable or intelligible behaviour, or into the standard patterns of anger or love, but the existence of such standard pictures shapes us in obvious ways. We act up to them; we keep what we can say of ourselves and what others will say hovering behind the details of our actions.

Closely related to this, the attribution of no single state can be independent of that of others. It is only with fairly large combinations of states that one can correlate any patterns of behaviour. And the behavioural signs of a state do not seem to be definitive of the corresponding concept. The behaviour associated with a psychological state, passion for example, may change over time. And it seems futile to try to tell when the meaning of the concept has changed and when people have changed their idea of how the state makes people act. (Homer and P. G. Wodehouse seem to agree on what passion makes one do. One might take this just as showing what passion has to be, were it not for other authorities, Madame de la Fayette for example, whose picture is entirely different.)

So the earlier 'behavioural' view has evolved into a 'functional' one. One standard philosophical account now is that psychological terms are understood as occurring in certain typical roles in the production of behaviour, and that, added to this, one has a large number of beliefs about how combinations of states result in action. In short, there's a theory of mind that we all have.[3] The theory may or may not entail eliminative definitions for some of its terms in terms of behaviour; there may be many sets of postulates that can generate it; it can

[3] The first stage towards the theory theory is found in some places in Wittgenstein, in Austin, and in Sellars. Putnam's and Fodor's functionalism represents an intermediate stage, and the most developed forms of the assertion that such a theory exists are found in Putnam's 'Other Minds', *Collected Papers*, vol. ii (C.U.P., 1975), and in David Lewis, 'An Argument for the Identity Theory', in D. M. Rosenthal, ed., *Materialism and the Mind-Body Problem* (Prentice-Hall, Englewood Cliffs, 1971).

evolve. The epistemological picture does not change much. One learns how to attribute psychological attributes to others and to oneself by seeing what one's elders say about people's actions, and, whatever routines one develops for telling what holds of oneself and others (they may be quite idiosyncratic), one refers back in doubtful cases to the orthodox opinions about what people do when in various states of mind. There's an epistemological advantage in the shift to the functional point of view, though. Since the attribution of a psychological state to someone need not be based on a definite conditional 'if this behaviour is found in this context, then state S is present', all that seems to be required is that the attribution of S to the agent under the conditions obtaining provides the best available explanation, in terms of what the attributer knows of the theory of mind, of why he acts as he does.

At this point the philosophical and psychological lines of argument approach one another. For the role of the 'inference to the best explanation' in attributions of psychological states is also stressed by psychological research on the matter. Consider what is known about attributions based on facial gestures and the like. Originally, researchers (from Darwin to Woodworth, say) looked for simple characteristics of static facial expressions that could be correlated with the various emotions (joy, sorrow, anger, etc.) that subjects claimed to be able to attribute when looking at someone's face. They looked for direct associations between faces and moods, as in Darwin, or, as on Woodworth's vastly more sophisticated approach, for patterns in the differences between different people's attributions to the same faces. Later researchers, trying to improve on these results, studied how longer patterns, including the background information available to the subject, and the information available in more extensive glimpses of a person as given for example by a filmed interview, affect the impression (accurate or not) that a subject gets. A third stage, now under way, studies the interactional dimension to attribution, the ways in which one's impression of another is based on his reactions to what one does oneself. The development through these stages has been consistently away from the simple linkage of traits and emotions to particular facial expressions or patterns of behaviour, and towards very complex models in which an impression of someone's mood or personality results from a mass of perceived and remembered information, only part of which concerns what he is doing at the moment. Moreover, it seems that even in very simple cases, when people have fairly uniform reactions to, say, a photograph, a lot of complex reasoning is actually taking place. As one recent writer, Frijda, puts it, at the end of a long summary of many of the facts and theories about the recognition of emotion, 'Recognition of emotion . . . often consists of conscious hypotheses and self-corrections, and it often involves explicit inferential activities, utilization of former experiences, and reasonings by analogy . . . It may vary from the immediately evident to the fully conscious making of plausible guesses.' As I would put it, impressions of personality are inferences to explanatory hypotheses.[4]

The drift of this, taken at face value, is that there is little that is psychologically unique in the attribution of states of mind. One has cognition, just cognition as it is everywhere, and beliefs, just beliefs, though they have a particular subject matter. The object of interest now becomes these beliefs and how they are structured. The standard view is that they are structured as an 'implicit theory of personality'. That is, as a body of beliefs, most of which everyone has, concerning the relations between different attributes. The dominant opinion is that the core of the theory is a set of roughly probabilistic correlations expressing

[4] See R. S. Woodworth, *Experimental Psychology* (Holt, New York, 1938); N. H. Frijda, 'Recognition of Emotion' in L. Berkowitz, ed., *Advances in Experimental Social Psychology*, vol. 4 (Academic Press, New York, 1964); J. S. Bruner and R. Tagiuri, 'Person Perception', in G. Lindzey, ed., *Handbook of Social Psychology*, vol. 2 (Addison-Wesley, Reading, Mass., 1954); Roger Brown, *Social Psychology* (Macmillan, New York, 1965); Erving Goffman, *The Presentation of Self in Everyday Life* (Allen Lane, London, 1967); A. Hastorff, D. Schneider, and J. Polefka, *Person Perception* (Addison-Wesley, Reading, Mass., 1970); F. Heider, *The Psychology of Interpersonal Relations* (Wiley, New York, 1958). Some more recent work, though not much evidence of recent progress, is described in D. M. Wegner and R. R. Vallacher, *Implicit Psychology* (O.U.P., New York, 1977).

the relative likelihood of a person satisfying one trait satisfying another. There is a good deal of evidence that people have fairly definite opinions about such correlations, and that they are relatively uniform from person to person.

When these hypotheses in the theory of attribution are combined with claims elsewhere in social psychology, for example in the writings of Heider, that people possess a conception of human action as caused by intentions to produce changes in the world operating with and against causal tendencies of the world itself, one gets the outline of a fairly extensive commonplace psychological theory, concerned both with dispositional traits such as those of character and mood and with the intentions that produce action. It is much like the theory that the philosophical writers have postulated—and there's evidence that it exists. It is surprising that no psychological writer, as far as I know, has tried to put the different parts of it, inferred in different parts of social psychology, together to see what the whole thing looks like.

BACKING OFF

A satisfying situation, one might well think: philosophical and psychological considerations work together, evidence backs up analysis. Certainly the virtues of the theories I have just sketched are very real, and must be exhibited by any theory that is to compete with them.

To begin let us see what variety of things can fairly be treated as theories. The central clearest cases are explicitly stated scientific theories managed by groups of co-operating scientists. There are also implicit theories, in which the people who share the theory share an unstated grasp of some crucial terms and assumptions. Nearly all theories are partly implicit. After all, Euclidean geometry went without formulations of some basic assumptions until Hilbert supplied them in 1899. It is essential to an implicit theory that if words were found for the silent concepts and formulations given for the tacit assumptions the result would be an explicit theory. The examples of non-scientific theories that I gave above, such as common-sense theories of child-raising or health, are surely largely implicit. (Are there wholly implicit theories? Much ideology, characteristically those parts whose falsehood becomes awkwardly clear when the belief is made explicit, must take this form. I think of racist or sexist theories implicit in our practices.)

Another contrast between theories is that between first-order and higher-order theories. First-order theories can be stated just as determinate assertions about a determinate set of objects and properties. Higher-order theories instead must be stated as assertions about properties of properties of the objects they discuss. Classical mechanics, for example, does not consist of assertions of the form 'objects move in these paths under these forces', or 'this kind of object acts in this kind of way'. Instead, it has to be expressed with differential equations, which say 'every object will move along some path, and here are some very general conditions on paths, from which you may be able to derive how a particular object may move'. The objects the theory talks about are objects with mass, their properties are their masses, the forces they exert on one another, and the paths they follow. A first-order theory of motion would describe directly the paths that objects take. (Aristotle's was a first-order theory of motion.) Mechanics instead describes some properties of these properties, in the form of a set of differential equations which, when solved, yield the simple algebraic equations one needs to describe the paths objects will follow. To put it differently, the higher-order theory says 'here's a classification of first-order theories, and under the following conditions the following first-order theories will be satisfied'.

Common-sense psychology is rather like an implicit higher-order theory, I think. And the parts which are implicit and the form of the higher-order principles make it very different from anything we naturally think of as a theory. The model on which I would like to construe the body of psychological beliefs is best seen in a linguistic example that is only marginally a system of beliefs at all. It is however a perfect example of what I shall call a *scheme*.

Consider the structure of the articulations we impose upon

speech. We explicitly classify stretches of sound as consisting of various words and as being sentences of various languages. Behind these judgements there is a system of unstated concepts dividing the words up into phonemes and assigning grammatical structure to the sentences. Jakobson's account of phonology and Chomsky's account of grammar are the classic admirable examples of how these implicit concepts and their relation to the actual discriminations we make can be analysed. Jakobson's phonology is particularly exemplary for my purposes.

There are degrees of implicitness of concepts. One explicitly labels a sound as 'cat'. Rather less explicitly, one takes it to be a string of phonemes [c] [a] [t]. And then at a level of implicitness that evades the vocabulary of most of us, one takes each element of the string as a complex of more primitive elements, Jakobson's 'distinctive features'. These elements are organized according to a system of relations, on Jakobson's theory a set of binary oppositions. These relations have a definite interpretation; they correspond to basic contrasts in the use of the vocal apparatus, e.g. vowel-consonant, voiced-unvoiced, grave-acute. (See the diagram on page 20.) Then one finds that in terms of this system of relations the complex of phonemes found in any spoken language forms a natural whole, and the range of phonetic systems corresponding to possible human languages seems to correspond to the range of simple complexes of sets of distinctive features.[5]

There is a general pattern here, that I would like to apply elsewhere, notably to common-sense psychology. We have a surface of explicit judgements, in apparent independence of one another, and beneath it a stratification of implicit concepts, at some point or points organized by some body of principles. I don't see any *a priori* constraints on what these principles may be. (Certainly, the fascination of Jakobson-like binary contrasts

[5] For the basic theory see R. Jakobson and M. Halle, *Fundamentals of Language* (Mouton, The Hague, 1971). I find Jakobson's *Child Language* (Mouton, The Hague, 1968) particularly fascinating. Chomsky and Halle's *The Sound Pattern of English* (Harper and Row, New York, 1968) brings out points I have ignored, for example the fact that phonology cannot be expressed just in terms of contrasts between features, and that we don't yet know what all the features are.

for anthropologists seems to me mysterious in view of all the other possible organizations of implicit concepts, provided for example by grammar.[6]) I need some terminology. I shall refer to a body of beliefs of this kind, including both surface explicit beliefs and underlying implicit constraints, as a *scheme*. So a scheme has adherents, just as a theory does, and can be taught and expressed, as a theory can be. A scheme consists of two sets of concepts and of beliefs. First there are the *explicit* concepts, for which adherents of the scheme have words. The beliefs are expressed in terms of them. Then there are the *implicit* concepts, in terms of which the explicit concepts are defined. Adherents of the scheme need not have words for them. They are subject to a *schematism*, a set of conditions on the ways in which the implicit concepts are related to one another and in which explicit concepts may be related to them. (Although I shall not directly discuss them, it is evident from this that a schematism introduces a yet more mysterious level of concepts, the relations (e.g. that of binary opposition) in terms of which the implicit concepts are organized.) The main effect of the schematism is to constrain the possible combinations of beliefs involving the explicit concepts.

Schemes may yet be simply higher-order implicit theories, for all I have argued. The contrast between schemes and theories must wait, though, while I make it a little plausible that there are schemes to be found in common-sense psychology.

DIMENSIONALITY

At each stage of the psychological theory of trait attribution one finds evidence that what is attributed in people's judgements of one another is not quite the same as the words used in explicit expressions of attribution. A revealing illustration of this is given by the few experiments in which subjects are shown photographs, or other data, of people and instead of being asked to

---

[6] Other 'structuralist' theories are in spirit closer to my project. In particular, theories of the constraints on plot in styles of fiction are presumably very relevant, given the connection there must be between an explainable action and an intelligible plot. See V. Propp, *Morphology of the Folktale* (University of Texas Press, Austin, 1968), and Claude Brémond, *Logique du Récit* (Seuil, Paris, 1973).

choose which of a predetermined list of terms fits them best are allowed to attribute states of mind to them in terms of their own choosing. Subjects then tend to mention the possible situation of the person and their possible actions. ('She looks as if she's watching her house burn down, and restraining herself from rushing in to save something valuable.') It seems from this that one's first reaction to photos and the like is to imagine whole complexes of thought, emotion, and possible action, that one could not express very succinctly in words; one imagines what the person's state may be like. Then, one tries to express this in whatever terms one has or is allowed to use. However the data here are not very extensive, and one should not put too much reliance on them. There are vastly more data on the attribution of traits whose description is given as part of the experiment. Then certain results, about what it is natural to think of as the dimensions on which subjects treat these traits as lying, are very well established.

The oldest data of this sort concern the 'errors' that people make in recognizing emotions as expressed by faces, etc. Though there is considerable variation in the attributes (from a given list) that are seen in a photographed face, say, the variations are far from random. As Woodworth, and after him many others, showed, the likelihood that a photo that one person takes to express emotion A will be taken by another person to express emotion B depends on the particular pair A and B. Some pairs of emotions are attributionally 'close' to each other, stimuli that evoke an attribution of one of them by one person are very likely to evoke an attribution of the other by some other person. And some are attributionally far apart; such paired attributions are unlikely. We therefore get a geography of emotions-as-attributed; the nearnesses are consistent if they are suitably arranged (so that, e.g. if A is near B which is near C then A is not too far from C). A good fit to a fairly large body of data is found in a five-dimensional arrangement due to Frijda. The dimensions do not have simple common-sensical expressions; they were obtained by ingenuity and sophisticated statistics. (But Frijda remarks 'if larger numbers of photographs and more reliable measurements could be used, chances are fair that more independent dimensions would be identified'.)

A very similar picture results from the studies of implicit personality theory. Although people's assertions and assentings and expectations do establish definite correlations between psychological traits, there are dimensional patterns to the variations between different people's responses. And, moreover, the primary data are probabilistic (subjects' judgements are of the form 'given T_1 the likelihood of T_2 is p'; the value of p takes some eliciting). There are thus degrees to the correlations, and an elaborate pattern of these degrees emerges. One impressive representation, due to Rosenberg and Sedlak, has four dimensions (the authors think that perhaps three would do).[7] (See the diagram on page 21.)

The most impressive thing about these studies is the number of traits that occupy spots on the maps—that fit into the correlation matrices. It seems overwhelmingly likely, at least to me, that in fact there is a potential infinity of traits that can be fitted into these patterns of correlation. In other words, that if the right dimensions are found and rightly interpreted every point on the graph, every set of co-ordinates, will represent a trait that can be intuitively taught and understood and attributed. The same conclusion could be drawn about emotions as attributed to pictures, and the like.

The central conclusion, for our purposes, is not that there are any particular number of dimensions to emotions or traits of character, or even that the system is a multi-dimensional space. It may turn out that instead of a number of dimensions one has a number of clusters, say, organized in different ways in different clusters. (Not only are there not enough data to settle this sort of question but, more fundamentally, one isn't going to settle questions of this sort just by fiddling around with observations and statistics. More general considerations are needed, in part of the kind that this book is trying to give.) The point to fasten

---

[7] See S. Rosenberg and C. Sedlak, 'Structural Representations of Implicit Personality Theory', in L. Berkowitz, ed., *Advances in Experimental Social Psychology*, vol. 6 (Academic Press, New York, 1966).

on is that there is a potential infinity of predicates (emotions, character traits, moods, etc.) available for common-sensical use, and that one's grasp of them derives not from learning them one by one but by having the ability to operate with a general scheme of attribution, which countenances more potential predicates than one actually learns or has words for. And it is organized around factors (dimensions, clusters, whatever) that are in general not themselves described in the vocabulary one uses to express one's judgements.

To be sure that the dimensions (or something like them) really do play an organizing role in our understanding of traits of character (and that we do not for example just have a great number of tacit theories of the various traits of character, correlating them in ways that accidentally happen to fall into a dimensional pattern), one could do a number of further types of experiment. One could, for example, invent words for co-ordinates to which no English character term corresponds. If these 'new' traits were easily grasped by subjects, and if they were related to each other and to existing traits in the way the theory predicts, then the dimensions would assume some psychological reality. It would still be extremely implausible, to me at least, that these dimensions represent a basic condition on the ways we can conceive of traits of character. For they were obtained from subjects at one moment in time from one particular (if rather broad) culture, they ignore all connections of traits of character with other states of mind, and they take no account of intuitively important common-sensical distinctions such as those between traits of character, moods, and emotions.

What I would expect is that a culture's set of character concepts would very often fall into a dimensional pattern such as these, though the labelling of the dimensions would vary from instance to instance. And I would not be surprised if the 'universal' conditions uniting all these systems of dimensions failed to be expressible in these terms at all, but rather required a more general understanding of the function of a character trait, as I begin to develop in Chapter VI.

TWO SCHEMES

Phonology

Explicit concepts	"cat"

various strata of
Implicit concepts

organized according
to schematisms

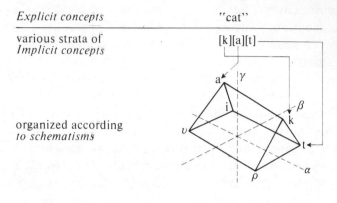

in terms of yet
*deeper implicit
concepts*

α = vowel / consonant
β = grave / acute
γ = compact / diffuse

which eventually
match up with
underlying facts
producing the
phenomena which
the explicit concepts
describe and explain.

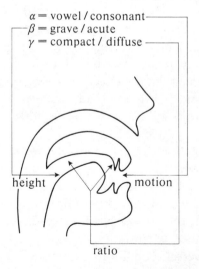

height →   motion

ratio

vain, proud, modest,...

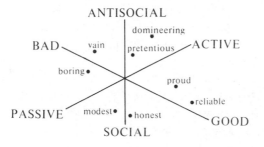

(a) good / bad, active / passive, social / antisocial
(b) each of these dimensions correlates, if Ch
VI is to be believed, with a way in which patterns
of explanation may be qualified, and thus
(c) the ultimate implicit concepts here are
those which underly the application of concepts
such at Belief and Desire, and the apprehension of
the conditions under which they will lead to action

The underlying facts (for the schematism of judgements of character) are thus
whatever the residue is of actual human motivational processes when we subtract
those which can be described in terms of items from the categories of belief
and desire. (See Ch. VI.)
(Diagrams distantly based on Jakobson and Halle, and Rosenberg and Sedlak.)

SCHEMES VERSUS THEORIES

It is not my intention in this chapter to establish that common-sense psychology is built round a scheme or schemes. If I can make it clear that there are two plausible alternatives, the scheme theory and the theory theory, and that the differences between them are important, then the rest of the book can present a case for the scheme theory in the only way that seems profitable. That is, by presenting a picture, a fragmentary impressionistic picture, of what the schemes in question might look like. The two great points of contrast between schemes and theories are in how they change and how they refer to their subject-matter.

It is a very subtle business, though, to bring out these contrasts, largely because the facts about how science works and about how linguistic and other schemes fit into our thought are so hard to be sure about. And I don't want to get drawn into the civil wars of the philosophy of science. It seems to me so clear that styles of psychological attribution and explanation possess an organization and undergo evolution far more in the way languages do than in the way theories do. And yet looked at in the abstract the beliefs that linguistic competence presupposes may seem to form a theory and the skills involved in adhesion to a theory may seem rather like those required for using a language. So the contrast slips away.

The most basic differences are those which determine the reference of terms in schemes and theories. Consider first some linguistic examples. The distinctive features of a phonological scheme denote those aspects of speech production which correspond to the distinctions between phonemes that they articulate; for example the feature *compact/diffuse* denotes the ratio of the sizes of the two resonating parts of the mouth when it is divided in two. If people learned another way of making speech sounds, so that e.g. the contrast between *k* and *a* on the one hand and *p*, *t*, *u*, and *i* on the other, did not correspond to the way the resonating chambers are divided (but, say, to the use of some prosthesis or special squeaker) then the *compact/diffuse* feature would come to denote the new and more complicated aspect of speech production. Contrast this with the situation if it was discovered that chemical compounds are not formed by the creation of complex molecules, but that instead though molecules do exist some other things are involved in chemical reactions, and all the assertions made in chemistry about molecules were really true of *them*. It is a very significant fact just that this situation is conceivable. 'Molecule' would not come to denote the newly discovered things; molecules would still be the little congeries of atoms they have always been. Chemistry would be in part false, though rectifiable just by replacing 'molecule' with a name for the other things.

Grammar is more plausibly scheme-like than everyday psychology, and less so than phonology. Very similar puzzles about reference occur with grammatical concepts. Consider Chomsky's idea that there are innate constraints on the forms that languages can take if human speakers are to learn them. If this is true there must be implicit grammatical concepts, one of the most general of which is 'well formed sentence of L', where 'L' is the language one is trying to learn. (What I will say applies, with suitable changes, to concepts like 'noun phrase', too.) The concept has a long history, but in this history it has denoted a series of languages, beginning with 'sentence of Zinjanthropusian' or the like, and now temporarily fastened on 'sentence of English'. It can come to denote the set of sentences of a different language without any change in the speaker's beliefs, for example if the environment of adults around a child changes so that a different dialect is spoken though the child cannot detect the difference.

Imagine as a limiting case of this a child who is raised by Martians who speak a 'diagonalization' of human languages, teasing the child by using before him a succession of more and more complex fragments, each just a little bit beyond his grasp of the moment. The child goes from false hypothesis to subtler false hypothesis about the form of L and about the extension of 'sentence of L', never getting it quite right. What *is* 'well-formed sentence of L' in this case? That of the Martians' sentences, that produced by the child's grammar at each stage, nothing at all? It certainly does not denote the extension of the grammars that were the original objects of the child's attempts. And it does not seem very plausible that it denotes the body of sentences forming the language at that moment of the child's tormentors, for it is not the structure of those sentences that is captured, or even with any justice aimed at, by the child's use of the concept. The reference of the concept is partially, and only partially, a completed business, by my intuitions. It reaches as far as some abstract object, a very general property of words which satisfy the child's cognition, and then gets no further. For it is an element of the child's thought, and one he cannot escape, that there must be a language L and that there must be a set of its well-formed sentences, but there is no such actual L and no such set. Similar, but worse, puzzles arise for concepts such as 'noun phrase'.

I don't mean to suggest that there is a definite sense to 'what "L" refers to' which some language meets or fails to meet. On the contrary, it is the indefiniteness that questions of reference take here that is my main concern. And I don't mean to suggest that this sort of predicament needs Martians to be realized. It is a real possibility, though I cannot find anyone who expects it, that the actual structure of English or some other human language not be describable in terms of the innate categories and modes of description provided by our language-comprehending capacities. We might produce sentences according to a pattern that in some rare cases and subtle aspects eluded capture by our grammatical intuitions. That is, our judgements about what is grammatical might not naturally project onto the set of sentences we actually produce. We will not be absolutely sure that this is not so until we have a grammar built on such intuitions that works for all of English. What then would 'noun phrase', or for that matter 'English' refer to?

Very abstractly puzzling issues perhaps, but the worry is not very serious somehow. A slight transformation of the question, though, makes it very real. Suppose that we are trying to tease out, not the structure of our language but that of our motivations and actions. The situation is more like that of the child confronted with a not quite learnable language. We move from one fragile guess to another, as cultures and styles of explanation change, about how belief, desire, character, and emotion lead to action and to each other. We are never in a position of being able to account for all the facts we are faced with, and we are frequently struck with facts that lead us to change our strategies for assimilating them. This clearly happens in the development of individual people and of human society. Can we be sure that these sequences of systems zero in on any truths?

There is a real possibility, I think, that we may culturally and even biologically be bound to modes of understanding that just do not allow us to integrate into our common-sense intuitive conception of the mental any general beliefs that are both literally true and describe the real causes of the events we use them to explain. The most striking thing, though, is that even if it is true (and it *is* very plausible of the body of principles available to many particular people) a kind of realism about everyday psychology is still possible. Particular explanations and attributions may still give the real why of particular actions; intuitively, they don't seem to depend on our possession of completely general truths, or on our being able to refer to causes that are operating beyond the case at hand. This is an intuition that is hard to capture if we conceive of common-sense psychology as a theory. Then what realism demands is that there be determinate properties that the terms of the theory refer to, and that the assertions of the theory be true when taken as being about these properties.

But the situation with linguistic schemes, and very arguably for common-sense psychology too, is different. There one can demand instead that for every explanatory context there be a set of properties and extensions satisfying the conditions of the schematism, such that the claims in question are true of them. Another context may demand another set. The presence of the constraints of the scheme prevents the weakening of the content of realism (from 'there are properties' to 'for every context there are properties') from being a trivialization. Thus we may preserve the intuition that even if different people spoke by use of completely different articulatory devices (as they do in a small way) the content of a particular phonetic judgement is correct as long as it captures a consistent way of applying the underlying pattern of English to that speaker's speech. Or that even if the causes of jealous behaviour vary from culture to culture and person to person one can explain a particular action by reference to the agent's jealousy as long as the underlying pattern in which jealousy and other mental concepts are connected can be suitably applied to the agent, so that what would in this case be jealousy is in fact found.

The point here is clearly very much like the extreme indifference of psychological concepts to the nature of their instantiations, that functionalist writers, especially Putnam, have stressed. The most basic neurological (or even functional) facts underlying the application of a concept such as Belief to me may be different from those which allow it to be applied to you, or to a Martian. And yet it does apply to us both just because in each case whatever does instantiate it satisfies certain constraints. Only, as functionalists seem sometimes not to see, these constraints may have to be articulated in terms of a different set of concepts to those whose application they constrain.

The general contrast between schemes and theories here can be put in a different way. The central role played in a theory by reference to the objects (properties, processes) the theory is about is played instead where schemes are concerned by the persistent presence of the schematism. A theory is made up of hypotheses which explain data, and the terms of the theory refer to those objects which lie behind the phenomena explained by the hypotheses, typically the hypotheses in which they were first introduced and typically the objects whose connections with the data are not too different from those hypothesized.[8] The presence of these constant objects unites different and sometimes incompatible hypotheses into one theory and provides the authority that lies behind each little hypothesizing. One can claim of one's explanation that it refers to objects which are also talked about, in a similar way, by other successful explanations, which are endorsed by many observers, theoreticians, experts. Similarly, the presence of the objects unites into one theoretical project different and sometimes incompatible people. All the

---

[8] What does 'lie behind' mean? Which phenomena? Which hypotheses? Until these things are specified there is a degree of agreement on this formula among different philosophers of science, and one seems to be able to get most interesting philosophies of science by spelling these things out differently. My own sympathies are with strongly realistic construals of these issues such as those of Putnam and Richard Boyd. But radically different theories such as that of Feyerabend seem to agree that a theory is held together by a shared conception of what it refers to, insisting only that this conception embraces most of the theory's assertions, so that the theory and its ontology change discontinuously at the slightest shift of doctrine.

subscribers to a theory share a basic conception of what its objects are, what phenomena they primarily explain, and how the theory refers to them. So the picture from the inside is that one's confidence of common reference allows one to judge the claim of a hypothesis to be continuous with or an intelligible rival to established doctrine. And the picture from the outside is that one looks at a stretch of smooth theory-development and asks how one can construe reference so that all these hypotheses are about the same things.

Schemes, on the other hand, are united by the congruence of each particular hypothesis ('that word was "cat" ', 'he's angry with me') with the schematism. Each hypothesis explains its data, or tries to, and each hypothesis refers to things that produce the data. But what things are referred to depends not on what produces the data but what facts the schematism is, non-accidentally, in the particular case, an adequate representation of. And the authority behind each explanation or hypothesis, the unity with the larger body of beliefs that gives it its plausibility and explanatory power, lies in the subscription of other adherents to the same schematism, and its past usefulness.

Theories and schemes are thus going to evolve differently. The come and go of particular hypotheses is not what makes schemes change, or what one measures this change by; instead, the evolution of schematisms and their changing modes of realization provide the significant differences over time. And their taxonomy will be different; one will group schemes into larger and smaller clusters, 'languages' and 'dialects', in accordance with their overlap not of particular hypotheses, nor of conceptions of and mode of reference to their objects, but of schematism.

THE HUMAN SCHEME

Two straightforward questions can be salvaged from all this grand abstract puzzlement. What kinds of facts are appealed to in everyday psychology? And in what ways can it evolve? It is perfectly clear that neither can be answered with any certainty at the present state of our knowledge. There are difficult factual questions here, about the nature of the thinking we do in attributing and explaining states of mind, and about the kinds of processes that actually produce the acts we commonly explain. These are knitted round conceptual questions, which I have summarized in asking for the source of the authority and unity of psychological explanation. Do we have in our patterns of explanation a bold conjecture of the culture, perhaps to be refuted some day and replaced by a different one?[9] Or do we operate less flexibly, and also less conjecturally, constantly improvising variations and improvements around some constants of what it is to take people as people?

The most striking thing about common-sense psychology in this connection is the combination of a powerful and versatile explanatory power with a great absence of powerful or daring hypotheses. When one tries to come up with principles of psychological explanation generally used in everyday life one only finds dull truisms, and yet in particular cases interesting, brave, and acute hypotheses are produced, about why one person, sometimes one group of people, act in some particular way. Somewhere in the works there has to be something very general and systematic, to back up these hypotheses. But it is perfectly clear that it does not consist in our having explicit general hypotheses of any great power available to us; they just are not to be found.

I cannot see that any general and systematic element, any source of authority for particular acute hypotheses, is to be had by our adherence to any sort of a theory. I cannot see where the shared conception of the objects of the theory, presumably our states of mind, is to be found, that makes us all subscribers. For one thing, people with radically different conceptions of the mental, dualists and materialists, bishops and their neurologists, can easily recognize the shared allegiance to a common-sense

[9] This seems to be suggested by Wilfrid Sellars in 'Empiricism and the Philosophy of Mind' in *Science, Perception, and Reality* (Humanities Press, New York, 1963), and by Richard Rorty, in 'In Defense of Eliminative Materialism', *Review of Metaphysics* 24, 1970.

conception of the mental, that allows them to discuss motives and characters. And if it was reference to the subject-matter that united different subscribers to a style of common-sense explanation, then one would expect to find both the extreme unconstrainedness of hypothesis and the safeguards against this freedom that one finds in science.

That is, theory is risky. It depends on a delicate balance of conjecture and fact, imagination and prudence, which the referentially based unity of the theory provides. Free imaginative hypotheses are allowable in science just because they take place within a network of tests, observations, and opportunities for critical reflection, that ensure public criticism of hypotheses and give refuting considerations a chance to appear. Science wouldn't work otherwise, without this organization it would be a collection either of dull empirical generalizations or of wild conjectures. Outside science, when one doesn't have this careful balance, one has customary belief, mostly empirical generalization and mostly true, and old-style metaphysics and new-style wild science, mostly conjectural and mostly false. Where could common-sense psychology fit in? It does not seem to be mostly empirical generalizations; beliefs, desires, memories, and regrets are too far from observation. And it certainly does not embody scientific balances and controls. Moreover the reason it does not embody them appears to be that it is not held together in the right way; one cannot be sure that what is being tested is quite what has been conjectured, and one cannot fit hypotheses together into a network of explicitly linked doctrine that ties theoretical terms to possibilities of observation. The explanatory contexts slide by too quickly and the connections between hypotheses never come near enough to the surface.

So we do not seem to have the benefit, in common-sense psychology, of the characteristic sources of a theory's unity. We do not have some of the liabilities either. We do not have to suppose that there is a one-to-one correspondence of our mental concepts with determinate attributes of anything, in order for individual attributions to be true, explanations apt, and whole schemes to describe some reality. There is, I think, a presupposi-

tion that the psychological explanations we make can be in some objective sense correct. And I would take this to mean that there must be some abstract pattern of properties and states and functions, to put it in cautious generality, which in any particular explanation can be hoped to find an instantiation in the facts causing the phenomenon explained. It is perfectly clear that there is only one way to argue that such an abstract pattern exists. I must try to dig up some intact pieces of the scheme and describe what they are used for. That is the rest of the book.

II

PSYCHOLOGICAL EXPLANATION

Explanations of human action, and of emotion, belief, and the rest of our mental life, are often very specific: they depend on the details of the agent's history, character, mood, all his mental and physical situation. They have to be, for slight changes in all these things can make great differences in what a person does, thinks, or feels. This is certainly a feature of explanations in one repository of common sense, literature. Think of Aida, for example; she knows that her lover, Radames, is going to be executed by being buried alive in his dungeon. She steals into the dungeon, so that when its entrance is sealed she remains to die with him. She had her reasons, which Verdi is pretty explicit about. She would rather die with Radames than live without him, and given this preference her action is not irrational. Yet it is not just the result of deliberation on this motive; it depends on the particular person she is. Another character might have wanted as she did, but have been too fearful or indecisive or conventional to have acted in the same way. Verdi knows this, and takes care to have shown earlier what sort of a heroine he has.

The specificity of psychological explanation creates a tension round a familiar belief about explanation, that it involves fitting a particular fact into a general pattern. What are the general patterns that are detailed enough to accommodate such very particular facts? One answer is to construe informal psychological explanation as centred on general patterns of reasoning, by which complexes of belief and desire result in action. I prefer another way, in part because too great an emphasis on reasoning and rationality diminishes the importance of the particularities of mood and character and situation that, I think, make psychological explanation often *real*—make it describe the actual reasons why people act as they do. In any case, the question here is, Where is the generality in everyday psychological explanation? And it is a good frame on which to hang a number of issues about the explanatory use of common-sense psychology.

EXPLANATION

Hempel's is the best-known, best-thought-out, best-defended account of explanation. The essential elements are a law of nature and a particular phenomenon that conforms to it. The example that Hempel always has somewhere in mind is that of an event explained by the laws of mechanics: the event is produced by the motions of bodies from an initial to a final position, and one explains it by deducing the motion from statements of the initial positions, the relevant forces, and the laws of motion. Hempel's statement of the general case is very familiar now; I only sketch it. One has a collection of *laws* and of *initial conditions*; from these one deduces a sentence *s* which describes the phenomenon to be explained. The laws cannot be just any general statements; they have to be 'lawlike', which means that they have to purport to express regularities due to the nature of nature rather than to accident.[1]

The emphasis on deduction, to relate the laws and conditions to the phenomenon explained, is essential. It allows Hempel to distinguish between partial and complete explanations, without having to suppose that any explanation provides *the* final, whole, unimprovable explanation of a phenomenon. For example, if we can provide laws and conditions from which it can be deduced

[1] See C. G. Hempel, 'Studies in the Logic of Explanation' in *Aspects of Scientific Explanation* (Free Press, New York, 1964). The necessity of explaining with laws rather than arbitrary generalizations was first pointed out by Nelson Goodman in *Fact, Fiction, and Forecast* (Harvard U.P., Cambridge, Mass., 1955), and the difficulties this poses for Hempel's account were pointed out by Sylvain Bromberger in 'An Approach to Explanation' in R. Butler, ed., *Studies in Analytical Philosophy* (Blackwell, Oxford, 1965). To some extent my reworking of Hempel's account is meant to take account of Bromberger's observations. Some difficulties of the application of Hempel's account to non-scientific explanation are described in Michael Scriven, 'Explanations, Predictions, and Laws', in H. Feigl and G. Maxwell, eds., *Current Issues in the Philosophy of Science* (Holt, Rinehart, and Winston, New York, 1961).

how a storm arose then we can explain the storm; but we may
not be able to deduce that a boat foundered in it. Understanding
how the storm arose gives one a partial understanding of why
the boat foundered—it is of explanatory value—but it does not
give enough for a complete explanation of it. On the other hand,
many other sets of true laws and conditions will, in general,
entail sentences describing the rising and storming of the storm,
and some of them may be more general, more fundamental, or
more interesting. This is surely as it should be; there is a
distinction between what explains and what is merely of explanatory value, and there may often be no best explanation of
a phenomenon. Hempel's approach yields both results.

   This outline seems simple and flexible; one would imagine
that it can be stretched to accommodate most explanations. Yet
it has seemed restrictive in two ways: in requiring that there be
general laws under which the particular phenomenon is sub-
sumed, and in requiring that the statements of the laws and
initial conditions be connected to the description of the phenomenon by a chain of strictly deductive reasoning. Hempel's
critics have often remarked on the restrictiveness of the first of
these, pointing out that if, for example, one explains a fallen
glass by saying that it slipped out of one's hands, one has not
stated anything like a law of gravitation. (And in explaining why
someone is weeping by saying that their cat has died one is not
stating anything like a law of motivation or emotion.) Hempel's
reply is that the law is not stated because it does not need to be.
Everyone knows that unsupported objects fall, so that what one
understands when one understands the explanation is that because the hands holding the glass did not provide it enough
support and because unsupported things (tend to) fall, it fell.
(And one understands that because the weeping person was very
attached to the cat, and because loss of objects one is attached
to tends to produce grief, and grief tends to produce tears, tears
were produced.) There seems to me something very apt about
this reply; but if we formulate it generally enough the theory that
results differs essentially from Hempel's official account.

   Consider the explanation of why a particular pane of glass

breaks when struck by a stone. Clearly the fact that the stone hit the glass at high speed and the tendency of glass to shatter when struck enter into the explanation. But one cannot use as law just 'glass breaks when struck', for some glass doesn't break unless struck harder than stones usually strike, and no glass breaks when struck as lightly as some stones strike. Evidently this glass was too weak to withstand this ball. One doesn't know more, often, and one doesn't know even this much until after the glass breaks. (So one could not have predicted what one explains, in cases like this.) Yet the result is a tidy Hempel-like explanation: the stone hit the window; the impact of the stone was greater than the endurance of the window; when glass is struck with more momentum than it can withstand it shatters. So: the glass shatters.

There are several morals to draw. Explanations often rest on facts that can only be known as a result of the phenomenon to be explained. Often, especially when this is the case, the law in question will be very inexplicit; it may say that there are conditions under which an event of the required kind will occur, without giving a very definite description of what these conditions are like. A strong enough impact on a weak enough glass will lead to shattering: a cruel enough loss of an object of sufficient attachment will lead to tears. A general definite way of putting the point is to say that an explanation need not state or name a law ('all unsupported bodies fall', 'Ohm's law') in order to *refer* to it, and all that is required of an adequate explanation is that it refer to, summon, the required elements—laws, relevant conditions, particular event—and indicate the way in which they are connected. One can do this without formulating the law at all explicitly; very often, and typically in psychological explanation, one does not state any law, certainly not as an explicit, definite, first-order generalization, and often not in inexplicit, allusive, higher order form either. Yet there has to be some law, some definite reason in the workings of things, why an event occurred in the way it did, which one can refer to in explaining it.[2]

---

[2] This account is compatible with whatever one's favourite account of laws of nature is. I would like to include it in a rather drastic revision of the idea of a law

If the theory of explanation is reformulated along these lines some apparent contrasts between different kinds of explanation cease to seem very basic. One such contrast is that between statistical and non-statistical explanation. A child has chickenpox and one explains his disease by reference to an epidemic of it among his friends. Certainly one cannot appeal to a law that all kids in these circumstances will catch the disease; not all of them will. Hempel would have one appeal to the law that such and such a proportion of children in the given circumstances will catch the disease, which induces a certain probability that the child in question will catch it. This approach is loaded with problems. (How probable must the event be? How is the probability to be interpreted?) Worst of all, it sacrifices the distinction between incomplete and complete explanations that Hempel achieved so tidily for non-statistical explanation: the explanation is better and better as the probability approaches one. One would imagine it to be better, from Hempel's point of view, to take all statistical explanations as incomplete, explanatorily relevant but not full explanations. Yet, it seems so clear that one has, for example, explained why that child has those spots on his face.[3]

The source of the difficulties lies in taking the law to be given by the regularity that such and such a proportion of children will contract the disease, simply because this regularity can be stated independently of the facts of the particular case. Inasmuch as one's explanation of why a child contracted the disease is correct, it is because the child was susceptible and the disease reached the child, though one could not have known these in advance. One is thus asserting that there was a medium of transmission and a category of individuals who will respond to

of nature, which disconnected laws almost completely from their statements in scientific hypotheses and empirical generalizations, but my purpose here does not require this.

[3] See C. G. Hempel, op. cit., Gerald Massey, 'Hempel's Criterion of Maximum Specificity', *Philosophy of Science*, 1968, pp. 43–7, and especially relevant for the view I am presenting R. C. Jeffrey, 'Statistical Explanation v Statistical Inference', in Wesley C. Salmon, ed., *Statistical Explanation and Statistical Relevance* (University of Pittsburgh Press, 1971).

transmission with infection. In using the statistical law as part of an explanation one is asserting this and also asserting that the transmission touched and the category covered the child in question. (Then the actual proportion mentioned in the statistical law has only an indirect explanatory force. If the proportion were too low one might not be sure that infection from the epidemic was the cause of the child's symptoms. It does not do any explaining itself.)

Some of the differences between psychological explanation and other kinds of explanation can now also be seen to be superficial. It is certainly true that we can rarely state laws of action, motivation, or thought, and that in spite of this we sometimes do pretty well at saying why someone did something. One manages to say enough that both one and one's audience believe of a particular operative principle that it, with various facts, is responsible for the phenomenon in question. One does this without stating, naming, conjuring up the principle. There is, I think, an enormous and shifting variety to the ways we devise of doing this, and a few constant patterns behind the constant improvisation. In the rest of the chapter I begin to describe these patterns. I shall try to stick to the quasi-Hempelian framework I have described. I shall take explanation to depend on reference to laws, and I shall take this reference to be something that can succeed or fail, so that the distinction between true and false explanations is independent of that between good (interesting, profound) and bad (trivial, superficial) explanations. I doubt that it is possible to give a general formulation of how reference to laws is accomplished, or for that matter how in general we refer to things in general. In the case of psychological laws I think the trick is turned by a nice combination of imagination, as I discuss it in the next chapter and Chapter VI, and the constraints on the form of psychological explanation that I discuss in the rest of this chapter.

EXPANDABILITY

We were looking for the source of the generality in psychological explanation. Now we see that we don't have to look for it in the explicit principles that people adduce in explanatory contexts, as long as we can show how they manage to refer to causally relevant principles behind actions and states of mind. A very basic fact about such principles, is that they depend very sensitively on the total mental state of the person concerned. Our patterns of explanation reflect this.

If I think that there is a tiger in the room I may well run out. But I may not run if I think that the tiger is tame and charming. And I may run if I think that it is tame and charming and carrying the plague. And so on. Principles like 'anyone who thinks that there is a tiger in the room will leave it' are, taken literally, almost always false. As a result, there are very few common-sense principles of the form 'if someone is in state s he will do a'. For someone in s and also in s' (e.g. s = believing a tiger to be near, s' = believing that any nearby tigers are harmless) may not do a. To put the point differently: there is no analogy in everyday psychology to the particles of physics moving under a known and limited number of forces. (It's all sublunary.) It is hard even to understand how one would complete a principle beginning, e.g., 'if someone were moved only by lust, then he would . . .', even in approximate form.

One has to take the agent's total state into account. One usually does not know what it is. Perhaps one never knows it all. One often knows enough about a particular person to say 'if he ever comes to believe that, he will leave the country' or 'if he thinks that someone has insulted him he will try to assault that person'. In these cases one knows that the agent's personality is such that whatever else he wants or believes or feels is not going to affect some one tendency to action. One very rarely knows this sort of thing about people in general. As a result, principles describing a general situation or state and relating it invariably to a consequent action are just not common. Of course we do know general facts about how many states (anger, lust, particular beliefs and desires) affect action, and the knowledge is expressed, in part, in principles telling ways in which these things affect action. They affect action; they don't effect particular actions.

So we must have principles concerning the ways total states of mind cohere, evolve, and lead to action. But we cannot describe (or even imagine, I suspect) total states of mind. There seem to be two possibilities. One is that we know principles involving very abstract properties of large states (e.g. conflict, inconsistency, support, coherence). No doubt this is true, and no doubt part of common-sense psychology looks rather like a crude metalogic or epistemology. But another possibility is also evident. It is that we have knowledge of a large number of possible transmutations of states, ways in which a state that is less than a total frame of mind *can* lead to another, if the transition is not inhibited by other psychological states or processes. One can explain an action by appealing to a chain of such transitions, that could have led to it. Why does one think that these transitions did take place? First because one has evidence that some particular inhibitions are not present, that one knows could block the transitions. Second, because one knows what action (or state) did result, and what the environment in which the agent is operating is like. For example, in the case of Aida one knows, roughly, that while in most people the realization that they would regret not having died with a condemned lover would not cause them to act as she did, because of timidity, conventionality, and a detachment from the impulses of the moment, in Aida these things were less likely to inhibit her action because of her passionate nature and—a point Verdi and his librettist bring out very carefully—a certain pride in not being mentally subject to the power of those to whom she is physically captive. So we have a desire, which would normally be blocked by certain factors, which are themselves blocked by certain facts about the agent. And when we learn about the action we get additional confirmation of her nature and of the terms in which she sees her love for Radames and her rivalry with Amneris.

There is evidently a close connection between this feature, expansibility, of psychological explanation and the general feature of explanation that I discussed in the last section. Psychological explanation has to cope with the dependence of action on the total state of the agent's mind. As a result, it has to be expandable: grounds that seem to explain why someone did something may be expanded to be part of an explanation of why that person did the opposite. One strategy by which everyday psychology can manage this, one which it clearly does employ, is to base explanations on possible, not-invariable, transitions between states of mind, situations, and actions, and on possible obstacles and encouragements to these transitions. Explanations of this sort will obviously not proceed by adducing general laws whose applicability can be known in advance. Rather, they must work by citing principles which may sometimes apply, which are usually known to apply only because of the event being explained, and which generate real explanations when the psychological facts of the case do result in the agent's total state of mind making a transition, one little part of which is described by the principle cited. This is the hermeneutical circle, perhaps.

EXPLANATION BY MOTIVE

People do much of what they do to get what they want. So one often explains an action by describing the agent's goal, and saying why he thought his actions would lead to it. Here, too, we find the expandability I have been discussing. And here we can begin to see the structure that makes these expandable explanations more than the impromptu guesswork that they may have seemed from what I have said.

The acceptability of motive explanations cannot be expressed just in terms of their conformity to some set pattern of practical reasoning. Consider, for example, the failings of a pattern like the following, which would lead to quite orthodox Hempelian explanations. Background conditions: agent a intends and continues to intend to bring about p. a believes that he must perform A by t in order to bring about p. a knows when t is approaching and is able to do A as t approaches. Law: agents do what they can to bring about their intentions. Phenomenon explained: a does A by t.[4]

---

[4] See William Dray, *Laws and Explanation in History* (O.U.P., London, 1964); G. H. von Wright, *Explanation and Understanding* (Cornell U.P., Ithaca, N.Y.,

The error is in thinking that knowing just this sort of condition and law will tell one *why* the agent acted on the desire or intention in question. Desires and intentions lead to action in many different ways, and if the action is to be explained the explanation has to indicate, refer to, the process that leads to the action. I think that when an explanation by motive succeeds it is because it succeeds in making such a reference, however formally perfect or imperfect it seems as practical reasoning. And I think that the form alone can be satisfied without there being a real explanation. Consider some examples.

The agent wants food and opens a package of sandwiches. Why not explain it as follows: he was hungry; he thought that by opening the package he could get at the sandwiches and thus satisfy his hunger; so he did it? We can certainly imagine the situation so that it fits this explanation. But we can imagine many things:

(a) *a* is running from a hungry lion; *a* is hungry too and stops for the sandwiches; the lion eats him.

(b) *a* is escorting his mistress into a French restaurant; they have been delayed in traffic so he is hungry, and when he sees the sandwiches he gobbles them up.

(c) *a* has just finished a large meal, when he is seized with a powerful urge to eat; he is puzzled, since the thought of food seems revolting to him, but he opens the sandwiches and takes a small, experimental, bite.

(a'), (b'), (c') same as (a), (b), (c) except that *a* avoids the sandwiches.

(d) *a* has brought the sandwiches along on a picnic; he becomes hungry; he opens the sandwiches and a chocolate bar, eats the chocolate bar, and gives the sandwiches to his dog.

(e) *a* has put a package of sandwiches in his pocket; his wife has substituted another, poisoned, and rather different-looking package; he gets hungry, reaches in his pocket, and opens the package, not realizing that it is not the one he placed there.

1971); I have learned from working through Lennart Nordenfelt, *Explanation of Human Actions* (University of Uppsala Philosophical Studies, Uppsala, 1974).

(e′) same as (e), except that *a* realizes the package is different and leaves it alone.

(f) *a* feels hungry and decides to break open the sandwiches; they aren't in his left pocket where he put them; he gets them from the bottom drawer of his wife's bureau, where she has put them after putting poisoned sandwiches in his pocket.

(a) to (f) (not (a′), (b′), (c′), (e′)) are stories which fit the explanation. But it doesn't explain them very well. For (a), (d), (f) the explanation is completely inadequate. In (a) one wants to know why *a* put his hunger above his life; his hunger alone cannot explain what he did. In (d) his hunger has nothing to do with his opening the sandwiches. In (f) his desire to eat falls far short of explaining his opening the sandwiches until one knows how he knew where they were. For (b), (c), and (e) the explanation has some force, but it is only partial; one wants to know more before one can say why *a* opened the package, (b) might be completed by describing *a*'s love for mildly anomalous behaviour or the acuteness of his hunger at that moment, or his inability to resist impulses. (c) might be completed by describing *a*'s curiosity about his own desires—his wanting to see what comes of following even the pointless ones—or by describing his belief that every momentary desire expresses a deep need of the body. (e) might be completed by a description of the package itself, stating its resemblance to the original one—so that he would not detect the difference—or by a description of *a*'s absent-mindedness—he wouldn't have stopped to consider any difference in shape and wrapping.

(a′), (b′), (c′) and (e′) show that *a*'s desire for food and his belief that sandwiches would satisfy it are consistent with his not opening the package. They can be expanded so that his hunger and his belief that the sandwiches would satisfy it are essential to explanations of why he did not open them. For example, in (a′) we could add that *a* thinks that if he satisfies his hunger he will no longer be in the state of desperate alertness that he must be in to escape the lion, or, that if he opens the sandwiches the lion, who adores corned beef on rye-bread, will run all the faster to get both him and the delicious-smelling sandwiches.

In all of these the reasons why the explanation is or is not adequate come down to the force of the indication of *how* the desire brings about the action. (a'), (b'), (c'), (e') show that the desire doesn't have to result in the action, by any psychological or logical necessity. In the first group of examples, (a), (b), (c), (d), the lack is that we do not know the motivational force of the desire. This is clearest in (d) where although *a* wants to eat and thinks that opening the sandwiches would allow him to eat, and although he does open the sandwiches, he does not open them in order to eat. Clearly, desire leads to action, often by complicated or subtle routes, and does not magically produce it, and clearly the explanation has to do something to indicate how this happens. In the second group of examples, (e) and (f), the lack is that we do not know the informative force of the belief. This is clearest in (f), where although *a* believes that opening the package will satisfy his aim, it is a complete mystery how *this* leads to his opening it. Clearly, the action has to be guided by information about the object of the action, and the explanation has to indicate how it is got.

So, when an explanation by motive works, when it tells you why an action was performed, it relies on an understanding of *how* an intention or desire moved the agent and how his beliefs guided him. This understanding can be given as part of the stated explanation, or it can come from what one knows about the agent and his situation.

A style or manner of psychological explanation, if it is to provide explanations that in this sense work, must have sufficiently wide resources that when motives lead to actions the route they take can often enough be traced by an explanation afforded by the style. And these resources must be sufficiently focused or apt that the explanations that they suggest are likely to be correct. There have to be enough explanations to cover the range of motivational processes, and there have to be few enough (or they have to be well enough catalogued) that the right ones can be found. The 'syntax' that I next describe enables common sense to produce a sufficient variety of explanatory patterns.

THE SYNTAX OF EXPLANATION

In fitting the general flow of desire towards action to the facts of the particular moment and person we have to appeal not only to standard transitions between states of mind but also to standard conditions under which transitions are encouraged or blocked. This is quite clear when we consider the resolution of conflicting desires. Aida presumably wanted both to live and to be with her lover. Dramatically, the second of these won. One might explain this simply in terms of the relative strengths of the two desires. One might explain it in radically different terms, too, as Verdi implicitly does. For someone else might have had all of Aida's desires, with the same relative intensities, and have acted differently. The reason would lie in a difference of character; Aida was passionate and impulsive and, most important of all, proud, and so she chose to follow love rather than prudence. Traits of character are involved, in much the same way, in people's differing willingness to take risks, or to act on impulse, or to think thoroughly about the consequences of different courses of action. It might be possible to produce an account of degrees of desire which managed to account for all of these in terms of the relative strengths of the agent's desires and beliefs. But it is clear that this is not the route that common sense takes.

Everyday styles of psychological explanation deal with all these things, as well as the ways in which people act on some desires and forget others, keep some in mind and turn others into idle wishes, are bothered and haunted by some while feeling a distance from others; they do so in terms of an elaborate structure of moods, characters, and styles. Most important of all, commonplace psychological explanation not only allows for all these, it often insists on them, to fill out the explanation of an action. They are not just trimmings.

It is characteristic of ascriptions of character, and of mood, that they serve this encouraging and blocking function. And it is characteristic of beliefs and desires that they provide the basic patterns which character, mood, and emotion, in subtly different ways block and encourage. We can divide the common psychological vocabulary into categories, characterizing them in terms of the roles that the terms in them play in typical patterns of explanation. This characterization has two sides. There is a 'syntactical' aspect, according to which terms in a category play a uniform role in admissible transitions, or of conditions on such transitions. For example with the categories *Att* of terms like 'enjoys', 'hates', and so on (understood as in 'he enjoys playing the fool') and *Act* of activities, there is associated the general pattern that I will write $Att \rightarrow Act$, corresponding to patterns of explanation saying 'he did it because he likes (enjoys . . .) doing it'. Of course other more complicated patterns are also associated with these categories, for example, $Att \rightarrow Attempt(Ac)$, corresponding to patterns such as 'he avoids doing it because he hates it'. For these italicized category names see the chart on p. 50. And of course there is the Classic $\beta, \varDelta \rightarrow Ac$, to correspond to the production of actions by the conjunction of beliefs and desires. (Note that $\beta, \varDelta \rightarrow Act$ is much less likely to be found.)

There is also a 'semantical' side to the categorization. With each category there is associated a typical manner in which explanatory principles involving terms of that category obtain their generality. For example, $Att \rightarrow Act$ principles associate with category *Att* a quantification over types of action: 'if someone enjoys an activity he may do it'. And $\beta, \varDelta \rightarrow Ac$ principles quantify over objects of belief and desire in a characteristically intensional manner, discussed in Chapter IV and its appendix.

One reason for the unlikeliness of $\beta, \varDelta \rightarrow Act$ principles is that the lack of a propositional content to activities, as opposed to actions, makes it hard to formulate general connections with beliefs and desires. Thus we can say 'he wanted an ice-cream and thought there might be one in the fridge so he looked for an ice-cream there' $(\beta, \varDelta \rightarrow Ac)$ and we can say 'he enjoys eating ice-cream and so he does it often' $(Att \rightarrow Act)$. But we cannot say 'he wants eating ice-cream and he thinks that there is some in the fridge, and so he is looking for it there', which would be of the simple $\beta, \varDelta \rightarrow Ac$ form. Note that we can say 'he wants to be eating ice-cream when she arrives and he thinks that there is some in the fridge, so he is looking for it there.' Here the antecedent is not of the category *Att*; rather, an item of the category *Act*, the normal object of *Att*, is being used as part of the propositional content of a desire. And, of course, the consequent is *Ac* and not *Act*. More problematic is 'he wants to be known for eating ice-cream in public, and he never knows when someone will drop in, and so he eats ice-cream often', which seems to connect beliefs and desires with activity rather than action. Perhaps it does; the example puzzles me. To me, though, the consequent seems not to be semantically an activity as much as an extended action; there seems either to be an implicit middle step 'he wants to be known for eating ice-cream in public, and he never knows when someone will drop in, and so he is always disposed to eat ice-cream, and as a result of this he often eats it', or the instantiation of a policy as an act, 'he wants . . . and believes . . ., and so he made it the case that he was often (found) eating ice-cream'.

It is not particularly important whether there are primitive $\beta, \Delta \rightarrow Act$ transitions. What I want the discussion of the question to bring out, though, is the importance of those connections of content which provide the generality of explanations and determine what items will fit together. Styles of common-sense explanation seem combinatorily pretty complete; if a transition makes sense in terms of the contents that it requires to be connected, then almost certainly a mode of explanation that contains terms of those categories will have some principle connecting them. (Just as in phonology if a contrast is required to distinguish two distinctive features then it is almost certainly to be found wherever it can be applied.) Certainly my simple arrow notation cannot express enough here. One wants something like: in context C (provided by a concatenation of states), states $S_1, S_2 \ldots, S_n$ lead to (or prevent the transition to) state S_m. I count actions and activities and the like as states here. Explanatory principles will generally have this form. But the principles are not definitive of the style of explanation; they are often improvised or alluded to on the spot given the immediate explanatory task.

Styles of explanation are given by specifications of the kinds of content states can have, and therefore the kinds of connection between states that can be allowed. These matters are discussed further in the appendix to Chapter IV and in Chapters IV and V. The immediate point is that the way in which common sense provides 'enough' explanations is by having a combinatorially pretty rich assortment of possible connections of content, and the way in which it allows this richness to be focused on the particularly cases (how there are 'few enough') is by allowing common-sense induction, apprehension of character, reflection on the act performed, and natural guile determine the principle to be appealed to in any particular case.

The summing up of all this must be more in the form of a claim than of an observation. The claim is that behind the body of psychological explanations that we use, or any other coherent body that others use, there is a fixed universal set of constraints, a less fixed choice of categories, and an even less fixed choice of psychological vocabulary and explanatory principles. The fixed universal constraints are that any style of explanation be expressible in terms of a choice of categories, and that explanatory principles take the form of permissible transitions and obstacles to such transitions between categories. A category is given by a characteristic way in which items from it contribute to the generality of such principles. Thus the category *Att* of attitudes towards activity contains terms which form principles which connect antecedent and consequent by a shared form of activity ('she detests travelling by bus, and so she'll go to great lengths to avoid going somewhere that trains or planes don't go'). And the categories of belief and desire enter into principles which are held together by their propositional content, in subtly different ways that I discuss later on. A category is thus given by a choice of generalizable content; to say this is not terribly helpful, however, in the absence of any general account of the content of a state of mind. A particular style of explanation is then characterized by a particular choice of categories. And the choice of terms, and of principles conforming to them, is characteristic of the 'dialect' or 'idiom' of explanation used by a particular group or improvised at a particular moment. How does one go about supporting a claim like this? Clearly not by trying to establish it *a priori*. Rather, one tries to show that the idea makes sense of varied puzzling things. Let me begin this task by working through one example, in an inevitably oversimplified way.

AIDA IN THE DUNGEON

Here are explanations of Aida's action in five different styles, followed by descriptions of some relevant features of the styles.

1: Romantic–Expressive. Aida, of a proud passionate determined nature, learned that Radames was to be left to die in the dungeon. She knew the fate intended for her, too, to live as a prisoner of the Egyptians, in the power of her rival Amneris. Fury at the indignity of this fate and passion for Radames led her to brush prudence aside and steal into his dungeon, to escape her imprisonment and rejoin him, if in death.

2: Rational–Calculating. Aida realized that if she did nothing she would live, in captivity, and Radames would die. She found this no better than not living at all, because she would be subject to the will of her enemies and separated from her lover. There was an alternative, to be with her lover and spite her enemies, which she found preferable, since it gave her autonomy and closeness to Radames. She therefore took it.

3: Social. Aida's jealousy of Amneris made the prospect of life as a prisoner of Amneris's father intolerable, and her frustrated love for Radames made her willing to do anything to join him. When the opportunity arose, then, to defy the Egyptians and join her lover, it suited both her jealousy and her love.

4: Deep–Symbolical. When Aida realized the fate reserved for Radames and for herself she was seized with a sense that Amneris's victory was complete, that as the Egyptian power was both imprisoning her and executing Radames it, an extension of Amneris, was taking him from her, imposing *its* death and thus having him, as she could not. His life could no longer be hers, but she saw that his death could be, if in dying with him she could make *their* death a frustration of the Egyptian will. And so she arranged their death, so that it was an expression of her choice rather than the Pharaoh's power.

5: Epic Primitive. When Aida saw her lover sentenced and saw herself imprisoned, anger rose in her heart and she said 'What I most want I cannot have, and my enemies triumph.' And she thought what she might do, to defy her enemies, and hid in the dungeon, striking their pride and stealing their victim.

In the choice of categories, terms, and principles making up each of these styles one finds some that are characteristic of them. Below I list for each of them (a) a category of psychological terms that is typical of the style of explanation, and (b) a typical characterization of the content of desire which permits the use of the terms in (a) in descriptions of motivation. Then I list terms that fall under these headings and describe the typical patterns of motivation appealed to.

In 1 the basic elements are (a) Psychical force: attributes of people which operate on types of situation to produce desires, and (b) descriptions of the contents of desires in terms of those situations which satisfy or thwart attitudes as described in (a). The terms are thus, will, temptation, pride, baseness, loyalty, and the like. Explanatory principles will be of the form 'someone who possesses attribute a will in situation S tend to desire d'. This style of explanation is suited to a moral universe in which ends are easy to see but hard to obtain, and what happens to an agent depends largely on his character. If the end is Good, character demands incorruptibility, will, perseverance.

In 2 we have (a) Reasoning—the production of desires from the interaction of the propositional content of other beliefs and desires, and (b) Desire—attitudes of comparative want to possible objective states of the world. The terms are the traditional philosophical ones: belief, desire, thought, means, end, intention. The principles are of the form 'desire for p and belief that q lead to desire for $F(p, q)$'. The generality of these principles consists in a quantification over propositional contents, and presupposes that such contents do attach unambiguously to motivational states. The style is suited to a moral universe in which ends are clear and means are obscure, and an agent's problem is typically to see his way to a satisfactory choice of the latter.

In 3 we have (a) Social relations—relations between people which dispose them to act in characteristic ways, and (b) Co-operativeness—descriptions of desires in terms of their conformity or incompatibility with the projects of others. The terms are love, jealousy, superiority, deference, and the like. The principles are of the form 'if people are related as R then they are likely to interact as P'. The generality is apparently simply one of what people in situations are likely to do, a quantification over situations and actions. In the appendix to Chapter IV I argue that something more complex is going on. This style is appropriate to a fairly primitive moral universe in which an agent's task is typically to achieve his ends consistent with the etiquette of his social situation and the demands of others.

In 4 we have (a) Symbolism—transient attributes of individuals which determine the terms in which they will represent a situation, (b) description of desires in terms of their symbolizability by realizable situations. Typical terms are, realization, insight, seeing-as. Typical principles have the form 'if a person takes situation S in manner M then they may act so as to make it representable as having property P'. This style is appropriate to a moral universe in which the situations and ways of thought of agents vary greatly, and their actions are only intelligible in the terms in which they pose them.

In 5 we have (a) Reaction—very general types of ends people are likely to achieve in various situations, and (b) Debate—desires are represented as being for particular objects, thought as a kind of action. Typical terms are assertion, struggle, revenge, and typical principles state 'if a person is in situation S then they will do a'. The generality seems to come from a simple quantification over actions and situations; to achieve more power the category of action is metaphorically extended. The moral universe here is one of success and failure for unproblematic goals.

In each of these the (a) and (b) parts fit together; the styles

Psychological category	Typical terms in our idioms of explanation	Typical logical form (very crudely)	Relevant parts of this book
Belief	believe, know, conjecture, think (**), imagine	propositional attitude (*)	Ch. IV and appendix
Desire	want, wish, lust for, desire, tend to (**)	propositional attitude (*)	Ch. V, esp. later sections
Attitude (*Att*)	enjoy, hate, yearn to	relation between agent and type of action	
Activity (*Act*)	skiing, fighting, making money	specification of a type of event produced or a type of experience	This Ch. (II), last two sections
Attempt (*Attempt*)	avoid, seek, try	relation between agent and a type of action	
Action (*Ac*)	names of particular actions	specification of an agent and of a resulting event	
Manner	quickly, slowly, with a club	adverbial: operators on propositional attitudes	Ch. III, last two sections, Ch. V
Character	honest, brave, evasive	relation between agent and situation	Chs. I, VI
Mental style	wilful, confused, pusillanimous	relation between agent and motive	This Ch., last two sections
Emotion	sorrow, distress, joy, expectancy	relation between agent and moment of time	
Mood	sad, impulsive	relation between agent and stretch of time (***)	Ch. VI
Intensional situation	love, hate, jealousy	relation between agent, referential relation, and object	Ch. IV, appendix
Objective situation	danger, chance, illness	relation between agent and environment	
Reasoning	thought, deliberation	relation between agent and sequence of motives	
Perception	sees, hears	relation between agent and perceptible aspect of environment	Ignored in this book
Memory	remembers, forgets, knows (**)	relation between agent and past thought, belief, perception	
. . .		. . .	

Notes: (*) These characterizations cannot distinguish between categories which are actually semantically distinct. Belief and Desire, for example, represent, according to the Appendix to Ch. IV and Ch. V, different relations to their objects.

(**) The overlap between, e.g., Belief and Reasoning, shows that the categories must ultimately be expressed with the implicit concepts.

(***) See Ch. VI.

are coherent. Each describes a 'moral universe', a mode of depiction of agents' situations, which embodies a guess about what in an agent's career is most likely to require explanation. The different styles are compatible; for any particular action all of them could be used to indicate the truth. And they are in another way incompatible; if one were to commit oneself to one of them as providing a central part of one's conception of human nature, then the choice of those categories and those processes as central would close off consideration of the categories and processes of another style as anything more than peripheral elaborations. Thus while 3 and 5 are in very little conflict, and 1 and 4 can tolerate one another, to choose 4 is to rule out 5 as an accurate depiction of the workings of desire. And to choose 2 is to reject 1 as a depiction of the relative centrality of character and desire.

III

IMAGINATION

By absence this good means I gain,
That I can catch her
Where none can watch her,
In some close corner of my brain;
There I embrace and kiss her,
And so enjoy her, and none miss her.
    (Sometimes attributed, probably wrongly, to Donne.)

People are unique among all the objects of our knowledge in one way; we *are* people. It is clear enough on anecdotal grounds that we exploit our similarities, both the little biographical ones and the deep essential ones, in innumerable incidental ways in describing and anticipating each other. And given the importance that some kinds of knowledge of others' minds must have had since the earliest days of human society, it would not be very surprising if the species and its cultures had developed systematic ways of exploiting our similarities to these ends. What one would expect is that sometimes one is predisposed towards one explanation rather than another of a person's action by considerations which refer to what one would oneself have done to perform that action. If there are such processes in our routines of attribution then if they are to have very wide application they must appeal to pretty basic and universal similarities in people. One might hope that these similarities are related to those which are expressed in the fundamental features of our patterns of psychological explanation.

Such hopes are satisfied, though in a way that now seems to us naïve and false, in the argument from analogy for the existence and content of other minds, as it is familiar from Descartes or Mill. The commonality of human nature is taken to lie in the universality of the basic elements of experience, and the transmutation of this commonality into beliefs about others is taken to lie in the potentially explicit and articulate projection to others of correlations between one's own experiences and actions. The two elements here that we find most indigestible now are the simple-minded inductivism—as if in supporting one's beliefs about others one could rely on no general beliefs about human nature but had to go back every time to the elements of experience and action—and the construal of the essential and universal attributes of mind as phenomenal, as ideas or experiences. More recent accounts of our knowledge of the minds of others are certainly free of these traits; but they get this freedom by abandoning the idea that understanding exploits similarity.

It is not necessary, I think, to abandon the idea. We can put together an epistemologically plausible picture of some parts of our knowledge of other people, and one which looks realistic from a psychological point of view, and yet maintain the link between particular guesses about the contents of people's minds and universal similarities underlying different human actions. The basic elements of the account, as I shall present it in the rest of the chapter, is that there is something reasonably described as a form of imagination that we can use to determine states of mind behind the actions of others. This imagination is very un-imagistic, though; it need involve no sympathy, no common feeling. Then the facts on which the justness of this imagination depends are represented indirectly in our system of psychological concepts by a constraint on psychological explanations, that they be imaginable, that they represent agents as passing through states of mind in a sequence that we can learn to simulate in imagination.

THE MIND'S MOUTH

Consider first a psychological hypothesis, though a very well confirmed one. It concerns the interpretation of the sounds of speech as speech, as composed of strings of phonemes. I am going to take this process, of interpreting someone's speech, as one of attributing a psychological state to them. I do this partly because it *is* a part, if a very rudimentary part, of many attributions of states of mind, and partly because if the over-all picture I am presenting is correct then what happens with speech is characteristic of something that can happen with attributions generally.

When one hears speech-sounds one interprets them *as* speech. One's belief that what one is hearing is, say, the consonant *s* is a hypothesis of a kind quite common in informal psychology. It categorizes an action, the speaker's producing a sound, as being of a certain type, not in terms solely of the result achieved but also of the manner and intention of production. We will see more exactly what sort of a hypothesis it is.

Suppose that one hears someone speak and takes him to be uttering the phoneme *s*. Suppose that one doesn't take it as a slip of the tongue; one takes the speaker to have intended to say *s*. It is a very ordinary attribution; it underlies others, and one may be hardly aware that one is making it. One might suppose that this is done in terms of fixed criteria determining what acoustical characteristics indicate an *s*. Or one might suppose that a sort of analogy is at work; one knows what motions of the air one produces when one's intention is to say *s*, so one attributes that intention to someone who produces these motions. The second of these is not particularly plausible here, but hypotheses of both kinds can be made about linguistic attributions at phonetic, grammatical, and semantic levels. But the truth about attribution of all these things seems rather different from either.

The truth about recognition of phonemes seems to be as follows. A short interval of acoustic energy can be taken as representing a number of different phonemes, depending on the sounds that precede and follow it, and the accent of the speaker. Some of the most striking examples concern the perception of tiny pauses: 75 milliseconds of silence inserted at the $\sqrt{}$ in *s*$\sqrt{}$*lit* will convert it to *split*, and inserted at the $\sqrt{}$ in *s*$\sqrt{}$*ore* will make it be heard as *store*. Similarly, a single burst of 1,440 cps sound is heard as *p* before *i* and as *k* before *a*.[1]

---

[1] See A. Liberman, F. S. Cooper, D. P. Shankweiler, and M. Studdert-Kennedy, 'Perception of the Speech Code', *Psychological Review* 74, 1967,

The data suggest a natural hypothesis, which by now is well confirmed. It is that one classifies phonemes in terms of the motions of the vocal apparatus required to produce them. Then when in the course of a string of sounds one hears another sound one already has a mental representation of the vocal apparatus set in a certain position, in accordance with the interpretation of the previous sounds, and then one classifies the sound one hears in terms of that motion of the apparatus which, starting from this initial position, will produce it. (More strictly, one interprets each stretch of sound as a sequence of phonemes which, interpreted as features of articulation, can be put end-to-end as conveniently as possible for the vocal apparatus.) This guess has had a good deal of experimental confirmation, and other 'analysis by synthesis' models are now common elsewhere in perception, especially in the perception of speech. It is certainly plausible that the general strategy for interpreting speech is to use an internalized representation of a (generic, probably) speech-producing apparatus, and to categorize the perceived input in terms of the instructions that would have to be given to the apparatus to make it produce it.

The general possibility that such accounts raise is that in interpreting someone's actions instead of operating from the data to construct a model of the psychological processes behind them one may do the reverse. One may use such a model, representation, image, to classify and articulate the data. This is the true sense in which the perception of a phoneme as a phoneme is a psychological hypothesis: one perceives the phoneme as being produced by an apparatus with a very particular, human, structure. Presumably, one's classification of many actions as being the actions that they are involves a similar sort of hypothesis: one perceives, classifies, and articulates them as being produced in accordance with certain mental processes. The important point is not the presence of representations of processes behind speech and action; one would expect

pp. 431–61, and J. A. Fodor, T. G. Bever, and M. F. Garrett, *The Psychology of Language* (McGraw-Hill, New York, 1974), Chapter 6.

them on almost any account. What one would not expect on many accounts is that actions, and speech, are perceived as they are because of a *prior* internalization of the psychology behind them. There is a kind of imagination at work, analysis by synthesis theories suggest, in which one understands what another does through simulating, imagining, how it might be done.

ACTIVE IMAGINATION

The mind's mouth is very different from the mind's eye. The simulation of speech that I have described provides mental representations of performances without there being any mental performances of any perceptual acts. It is this quality of non-imagistic imagination that I think is found elsewhere in our interpretation of action. Let me build up to it gradually, in part because I want it to be clear that what I am presenting is an epistemological theory as well as a psychological speculation.

If one is planning to do something one often rehearses it mentally. Perhaps one always has to have some form of mental rehearsal, if only to get the sequence of actions co-ordinated. Such a rehearsal requires that one mentally go through some simulation of the actual performance. This clearly need not involve simulation of perception, but clearly it may in some cases involve it, for example when the exact manner in which the action is to be performed depends on what one sees happening after one has begun to perform. (One can't prepare what one will say to someone without imagining what she might say back.) One can rehearse someone else's actions, too, sometimes overtly, as with a child watching a film who punches the air as the hero fights with the villain, and sometimes covertly, as with the child's parent at the same film who only mentally punches and reels.

In imagining a fight one is imagining the actions of at least two people. The imagining cannot be a mental re-creation of observations of the fight. For one can imagine the fighter's motives and thoughts; one may sometimes have to, to be able mentally to fight in the right manner. And there is a certain perspectivity to imagination: one imagines the fight either from the position of one fighter or from that of a bystander.[2] This perspectivity is not an optical matter; it is independent of the geometry of any images one may have. It is a matter of, to put a label on it, thinking as if from inside one or another participant. It seems to me that these obviously related features of imagination, the imagination of thoughts-in-action and the perspectivity of imagination, are smoothly explained by the hypothesis that the core of imagination of actions consists in their simulation, as if one were practising to perform them oneself.

One cannot imagine actions without imagining thoughts and perceptions also, since one may be imagining the action as formed by a changing environment, which is perceived and reckoned with. And so to the extent that one represents the *complete* production of the action one represents the agent's perception and thought too. I doubt that the representations of action that I am concerned with are very complete, though, and thus I must explain, among other things, the truncated representations of thought and perception that they involve. Such representations seem necessary for the perspectivity of imagination, since it seems to require, in fact to consist in, some objects of imagination entering as simulated actors and some as objects of information used by these actors.

It hardly seems controversial that we do imagine the situation of others, or that this imagination is partly imagistic, partly not, and usually perspectival. Yet there need not be any unity to these imaginings; they may just be a collection of consequences of the vast, complicated procedures by which one gets one's opinions about others. For the imagination of action to be a fundamental and studiable thing, it must be constrained in some definite ways. The range of representations of actions in imagination must be somehow limited to a special subset, which

[2] See Richard Wollheim, 'Thought and Passion', *Proceedings of the Aristotelian Society*, 68, 1968, pp 1-24, and 'The Mind and the Mind's Knowledge of Itself', *International Journal of Psychoanalysis* 50, 1969. I have heard similar ideas attributed to Bernard Williams.

possesses the right kind of autonomy. The imagining we need must be independent of other sources of knowledge about mind and action, as much as possible, and as much as possible must not involve substantial simulation of thought and perception, while retaining enough reference to them to support a perspectivity. It has yet to be made plausible that such a process can exist.

SIMULATION AND ACTION

To see how actions may be simulated, begin with how they are performed. I make two assumptions about action. First, that actions can be learned; one can put new actions into one's repertoire, and change the manner of performance of established actions. Second, that actions are guided by information about the environment and about the purpose of the action; one doesn't act just by withdrawing a discrete act from one's repertoire and sending it out into the world, for what motions one makes will usually depend on how things develop during the performance. Theories of action (of skills, of motor learning) that satisfy these two conditions cannot differ very much from what are, in psychology, called open-loop theories with stored schemata, that is, theories according to which the specifications of an action are held in memory as descriptions of fairly general ways of initiating the action and of the expected or intended effects on the agent's body and the environment.[3] The action is then carried out by a process that generates suitable motions in accordance with continuing perception, to achieve the right result. What is important for our purposes is that actions result from the (intentional or non-intentional)

---

[3] See J. A. Adams, 'A Closed-loop Theory of Motor Learning', *Journal of Motor Behavior* 3, 1971, pp. 111–50; Richard A. Schmidt, 'A Schema Theory of Discrete Motor Skill Learning', *Psychological Review* 82, 1975, pp. 225–60. This work seems to me to be rather close to criticisms of behaviouristic accounts of action which J. A. Fodor presents in 'Explanations in Psychology', in M. Black, ed., *Philosophy in America* (Cornell U.P., Ithaca, N.Y., 1965). I was therefore startled to find that later work of Adams presents an account of the timing of actions that, if what I say in Chapter IV is correct, undermines their common-sense structure.

putting into effect of (remembered or invented) descriptions of what one wants to do, and that in the actual performance of the action the details of it get specified in accordance with the developing situation. The consequences of this point of view for the concept of action are quite substantial; in Chapter V I shall argue that it is at the heart of what it is to conceive of action as action, rather than as behaviour or motion.

So let us take action as resulting from a set-up roughly like the diagram on p. 60. The model does not need any modification to allow some kinds of imagination of action. It most explicitly allows the imagining of one's own actions. The crucial element here is the function of memory. Suppose that one is thinking out a future action or rehearsing an instance or variation of a habitual action. One draws from memory a description of the action—one remembers what to do—and one develops it towards performance, seeing how one would or will perform it and stopping short of final execution. The process is fairly described as imagination because what is remembered is the action as performable, that is, as an outline specification to be filled in during performance; what one remembers is not just a performance minus the innervation of the body, since this would miss the schematic quality that allows one to adjust a perform-ance to the details of the situation, and it is not a *verbal* repre-sentation of an outlined action, since one can almost never verbally describe the crucial features. As a result, the memory of the action can be 'read out' according to various possible contingencies, to give more detailed specifications of the action as it might be performed. It is to get these more detailed specifications that we do rehearse and anticipate. To the extent that it is a suitable object for respecification and evolution the remembered action embodies a body of implicit conditional facts; if the situation were like *this*, the action would be done *so*.

Psychologically speaking, this amounts to the claim that skills are stored as instructions for correlating sensory (and muscular) feedback with control over the muscles. They thus contain representations both of sensation and of motor control, both are 'coded in'. (Presumably, it doesn't say what to do

HOW TO IMAGINE AN ACTION

Evolution of content:

Possible instantiation:

A

Action as end
to be accomplished

B

Redescription of action
in terms that can guide
performance, as a formula
for co-ordinating perception
and bodily motion towards
the end. Action as behaviour.

C

Specification of this
formula in terms of
particular perceptions and
motions, either in response
to actual information in
action or just by attention
to one particular 'reading'
of it. The result is action
as motion.

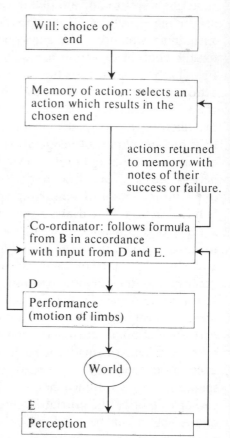

Two ways of imagining action:
  (1) (see pp 58–62) Remember an action (B) and specify it (C) in accordance with
      information from perception, or just specify it in accordance with *possible*
      perception. The second of these does not require that the possible perception
      be imagined. This is so because, psychologically speaking, the connections
      between B and C are independent of A, D, and E, or, more abstractly,
      because actions-as-co-ordinations are neither actions-as-accomplishments or
      actions-as-motions.
  (2) (see pp 62–6) Remember an action and vary the specification (as in (1)) of it,
      until the simulated result matches some models of comparison. Return it to
      memory and repeat the procedure until a description is drawn from memory
      which when specified has the required properties. This is only possible when
      an independent characterization of the target, in the vocabulary of C,
      is available.

given *any* sensory or motor feedback, but only given 'anticipated' results. If something peculiar happens, then one has to
stop and think what to do.) Then, when an action is being
mentally rehearsed, before being performed, the remembered
specifications of the action are read out in accordance with one,
or more likely several, possible sensory–motor plots, and
adjustments are made between the specifications and the ways
they are used (between B and C) in order that when the action
is actually performed all will go smoothly. (Perhaps somewhat
different ways of performing the action are tried out and
compared. Perhaps some details of timing and effort are
settled.)

In terms of the common-sense conception of action, what is
essential here is that one core element of that conception, that
actions result from the instantiatiation of generic intentions,
presupposes facts about the production of action which can
naturally be exploited in such processes as planning and
rehearsal to give fairly full simulations, imaginings, of actions.
And this simulation can be an autonomous affair, though
certainly nothing I can say will show that it has to be. At any
rate we have here a way in which this imagination can proceed
without the full resources of self- and other-knowledge. In
particular it need not require that in imagining an action one
imagine the perception or thought that accompany it, one may
just run through the action as remembered, developing it in one
of the ways it allows, with perception and thought items left
blank, identified only by the place that is left for filling them in,
rather than clumsily producing representations of a whole
complex of mental states. I find it appealing to suppose that
this is usually how the imagination of action works, but the
evidence lies more in the phenomenology of rehearsing and
anticipating than in any really solid theoretical considerations.
One seems just to think what one may do, and then when one
does it one finds the performance as one had expected while the
experience is novel, not part of what one had prepared for.

An example: suppose one is playing music from a score.
What one remembers is some general instructions about how

to use one's instrument and the method of responding to the printed notes so as to produce the music. One can do long stretches without thinking about it; some stretches—runs, arpeggios—can only be done as routines learned in advance. One can look ahead and decide how one will play a passage, and then rehearse it mentally. When one does so one does not necessarily imagine the sounds that are to be produced, but one does imagine oneself, for example, controlling the pitch (on strings or wind instruments) in response to what one's ears tell one about one's sharpness or flatness. (Without imagining the sound! If this is a paradox, get used to it!)

NARRATIVE IMAGINATION

So far, so good, perhaps, but by 'imagining an action' I meant in the last section 'imagining oneself performing an action', and surely the most interesting cases are those of imagining someone else's actions. And there seems to be an obstacle to connecting the rough description I gave of how one can imagine, for example, a fight between others, with the model of rehearsing and simulating of the last section. For it would seem that in order to imagine another's action on that model one would have to be able to draw out of one's repertoire the action as performed by him; one would have to remember how to do another's action. This seems false, in many cases.

I think that there is a real obstacle to imaginative understanding of another here, rather than a failure in a theory of it. It *is* hard to imagine actions one doesn't or cannot perform. And there could well be creatures which imaginatively rehearse actions but cannot imagine actions as performed by others. (I would suspect that cats were such creatures were it not for their capacity to imitate one another.) The obstacle is overcome, though, in varying degrees. The basic ways of overcoming it lie in the flexibility and universality of the action-producing apparatus.

Though one's repertoire of actions is inevitably limited, the procedures by which one produces them are essentially those which other people use when doing things not in one's repertoire. We expand our repertoires when we experiment or imitate or follow instructions. When one succeeds in doing something one remembers some schematic image of what one has managed to do and stores it away for future use. This common-sense fact about learning is easily incorporated in the model of the production of actions. The description of an action that one remembers and then specifies in performance can be remembered again with a slight expansion; now it must be described as also a means to the end which it was perceived as accomplishing. And, somewhat more problematically as I discuss below, one can also add to the description some note of how it is to be specified to get the result.

The result is another form of imagination. For now one can mentally enlarge as well as mentally rehearse one's repertoire; one can begin with a very elementary description and then proceed to develop and vary it in simulated action, just as in rehearsal or anticipation, while noting, keeping track of, the results of the experiment, until something is obtained which matches some object of comparison. One rehearses an imitation in this way, practising it mentally until one gets it right, and one guesses how someone does something by beginning with an idea of an action of one's own and modifying it until it approximates to the target. (See the diagram again.)

ANALYSIS BY SYNTHESIS

It is essential to see that what we have in effect done at this point is to re-create the idea of analysis by synthesis from a development of a commonsensical conception of action. For we can now describe the analysis of a perceived object (action, word, or whatever) as follows. Faced with the object one remembers actions that could result in something similar. Then one 'performs' them mentally with experimental variations. That is, one proceeds as one would if performing the action, controlling the details of one's performance in accordance with one's perception of the results, but with the difference that one cuts off the action from actual implementation and continues the comparison with 'results' given not by what one has done but by the object of analysis. One does this with different initial action-descriptions and different ways of specifying them until one gets the congruence that in actual performance would count as success. In short: the object is analysed in terms of the description-for-performance of an action such that its performance, cut off from actual muscular motion, and the perception of the object fit together to give just the congruence, the sense of controlled action and successful result, that a real performance would.

To say this is not to make any claim that what one does in perceptual analysis by synthesis is to use any of one's actual capacities to action. The real facts are probably much more complicated than that. Rather, the point is that there is little in the idea that is not already in the idea of a controlled learnable action. One interesting consequence of this arises from the fact that analysis by synthesis inevitably introduces the idea of an internal code into which perception is analysed, what J. A. Fodor calls a 'language of thought'[4]: the action-as-perceived is encoded, characterized, redescribed in terms of what it would take to produce it. This technical psychological idea, then, that some thought can be described as the manipulation of symbols in a language that no one speaks, while clearly conjectural and risky, is hinted at in common sense. One shouldn't be surprised when in everyday life descriptive metaphors and on-the-spot conjectures seem to appeal to something like it. If you can do what you intend and if what you intend isn't always something you can exactly say, and if you can compare what you do with what you wanted to do, then you can understand things you haven't the words for, by knowing what you would have to be up to to produce them.

The most basic and intuitive sense in which these processes are rightly called encodings (language-like expressings, conceptualizations) is that they result in a representation whose temporal ordering is not the same as that of its object. Things get

---

[4] See J. A. Fodor, *The Language of Thought* (Crowell, New York, 1976), especially Ch. 1, and also Ulrich Neisser, *Cognitive Psychology* (Prentice-Hall, Englewood Cliffs, 1967).

collected together and rearranged. And the parallel between the conceptualization of experience and the control of action is striking in just this respect, too; one intends that certain ends be accomplished, that one's mouth form the sounds of 'cat' for example, and then in performance these intentions are 'translated', 'decoded' into actions whose parts, for example the movements of tongue and larynx, have a different temporal arrangement. And in these terms too, imagination preserves its puzzling status of being neither perception nor thought but somewhere in between. What passes during imagination is arranged in time in a way that assimilates it neither to perceived events nor to conceptualized thoughts. One imagines the word 'cat', and one finds that one is not in the presence of any elements ordered in the way the sounds, the acoustic signals are; it's striking how one *cannot* imagine that. But neither does one just have a thought of 'cat', not even a thought of those phonemes in that order. Neither ordering and neither manner of conceptualization is right, and evidently this is not because one has something else or a little bit of both, but because what one has is a re-creation of the process of going from the one to the other. In imagining the word 'cat' one is running through the routines of managing muscular control and sensory information that would be required either to say the word or to decipher it from heard speech.

Imagination is hard to imagine, then, though thought is repeatable, packaged in its symbols, and images are imaginable, susceptible to having the processes by which we assimilate them re-created. Much of what I have been calling imagination must consist of automatic, fixed or learned, routines of matching perception and conception. Standard unproblematic voluntary action, the perception of speech, and much of one's day-by-day interpretation of people's actions as actions, must take this form. The codings and decodings just happen, and we don't have much control over them or ability to re-create what goes into them. But sometimes one acts in a way that is idiomatically more 'imaginative'. One understands someone's speech or manner well enough to imitate it, or one senses the expressive character of what someone is saying or doing. When one can do this one must be exercising some control over the processes of interpretation and correlation that one normally performs automatically. To the extent that one has this control, and it is always very limited, one can after practice or mental rehearsal modify one's remembered description of an action so that it now includes some specification of the exact style in which it is to be performed.[5]

CONSTRAINEDNESS

It is important to see how constrained a business this re-creation of an action is. One has to start with something one can do and then vary it. There seem to be two possibilities for imaginative variation. One can take very simple actions and put them together in new ways, synthesizing the desired action like a laboratory synthesis of a natural chemical. Or one can take a complex action and vary it. Various basic modes of variation are represented in common-sense adverbial idioms; one can do the same action more quickly or hastily or with a club.[6] I would imagine that there is a lot of information about these matters contained in the descriptions of action in our languages, more, in fact, than just the classification of adverbs as representing modifications of time, place, instrument, and so on. A good example both of the difficulty of imitation and of our uncanny ability to do it is the learning to pronounce a foreign language. At first one imitates the foreign sounds by doing the variations of sound one's own language permits, and while the results of this are always imperfect it can often be clear enough what it is one is trying to reproduce. Then as one gets better at it one learns to modify not the final English phonetic acts but more nearly atomic phonetic performances, until eventually one

---

[5] The ability to parody or caricature clearly requires this kind of control. And the parodies or caricatures themselves are interesting for their quality of being too close to be likenesses; instead they represent instructions of how to imagine the person or voice or manner in question. They are attempts to articulate these mysterious elements of imaginative control.

[6] The importance of the modification of descriptions of action by our stock of adverbs was first noted by Anthony Kenny in *Action, Emotion and Will* (Humanities Press, New York, 1969).

produces actions that branch from any English performance at a pretty basic level.

The constrainedness of the imagination of action is its most striking feature. Strangely, this gives it its power and independence. One can imagine actions one could not actually perform —watching someone dance one can imagine doing it like that— because one does not have to imagine *all* the control over muscles and use of perception. What one imagines represents the act it is an imagination of, and to that extent it must have an accurate schematic resemblance to the original. But the schema need not be developed in all its details, and essential elements may be left blank. As I said earlier, this constrained quality is also responsible for the autonomy of the imagination of action. Some of the sources of this autonomy are easiest explained through another example. A music student is taking a lesson. As he plays a passage something goes perceptibly wrong, and after puzzling over the event for a moment the teacher says 'That F sounded terribly pinched, and you missed the crescendo; I think you must be worried you may go flat on the B that follows it, and so you're correcting in advance and in the wrong way, by squeezing the reed; here's what you sound like . . .' And then she plays it as he did, only even worse, followed by a correct execution, so that he can begin to hear the difference.

The teacher has come up with a guess about what the student did, both of what invisible motions he made with lips and breathing and what lines of thought lay behind them, by imagining a mistake she never makes, perhaps never has made. To arrive at her guess she has to take the sound she hears the student produce (a cramped F followed by a too quiet but surprisingly on-pitch B) and describe it to herself. She has to think of it in terms of the categories she uses to regulate her own playing: sharp–flat, full–cramped, loud–soft. Then she has to mentally play the passage with this result in mind, to see what manner of execution may produce it. After she has convinced herself of the situation, she cannot just tell the student that the trouble all comes from trying to control the pitch with his lips more than with his breathing; she has to make him hear the relevant contrasts between sounds that allow her to classify them so usefully. And so she plays him both the wrong and the right way, until he can hear the difference.

We see here both the autonomy and the constrainedness of the imagination of actions. A central part of the teacher's thinking consists in mentally varying a mental performance of the passage until it fits a certain description. But this description had to be given; it had to be obtained in some other way. And the ascription of further states of mind on the basis of her imaginative exercise, the supposition that it was nervous anticipation of the B that made him tighten up on the F, is also not given by it. The imagination of action must be framed on two sides, on the one side by an essentially inductive classification of perceived actions, and on the other side by hypotheses, influenced by theory and culture and no doubt by other mysterious kinds of imagination, about the nature of the mental. It requires both, and serves to prepare the former for the latter.

'Analysis by synthesis' processes like that I have been describing, in which something perceived is analysed in terms of what one could do to produce it, are probably very common. Their particular appeal in the psychology of language is evident. We find there a wonderful combination of a fixed schematism, the Jakobsonian features, which has an obvious interpretation in terms of the mechanisms of speech production, and an impressively apt analysis of the production and analysis of speech. There is an inevitable connection between the existence of a schematism and the possibility of such 'imaginative' procedures, for the schematism provides a limitation to the otherwise endless array of possibilities that one would have to search through to find a match for a given target. In the form of imagination I have been discussing, the schematism is provided by the conception of actions as resulting from the successive 'rewritings' of initial 'descriptions'. In Chapter V this idea is developed into a not at all innocuous form, and turns out to be important to the concepts of belief and desire.

There are many others parts of the psychological schematism, and I am sure that some of them too are associated with analyses by synthesis. Not everything of this general sort can plausibly stand as a form of imagination. The core of imagination, in the attribution of states of mind to others, is this mysterious business of acting out stories to oneself, part of which I have been trying to elucidate. Puzzling as it is what the general features of this narrative imagination should be, two seem fairly clear. First, there must be a quality of perspectivity; there must be a difference between being simulated as an actor and as an object of action. And second, the ability to imagine part of an agent's state of mind must provide one with some knowledge of what it is like to be that agent (in that way at that time).[7]

I am certainly not going to try to analyse either of these problematic notions, perspectivity and 'what it is like'. Some aspects of their use are clear enough, though. When one knows what it is like to be in a certain situation or state of mind one is able to take purported explanations of the actions of an agent in that situation or state and see if they apply. One can mentally test them, seeing if that state really does lead to that situation. Attributions of character play a role in explanation very similar to this, as I argue in Chapter VI, and thus it is not surprising that knowing what it is like to be someone (in a certain respect at a certain moment) is commonly taken to give one insight into that person's character, or mood or emotion.

Rather than pretend to have an understanding of narrative imagination, or of knowledge of what it is like to be another, that I do not have, I would like to end the chapter with some remarks on what these things do not entail. Most strikingly, they do not seem to entail that in imagining someone's situation one must have or get any understanding of the phenomenal quality of that person's experience. The level of thought involved

---

[7] The terminology of 'what it is like' was introduced into philosophy by Thomas Nagel in 'What is it Like to be a Bat?', *Philosophical Review* 83, 1974, pp. 435–50. The phrase has assumed a life of its own, in the typical Quinean way, since its introduction, and many of us now have intuitions inconsistent with Nagel's, which we express using it.

seems to be neither verbally conceptual nor imagistic. I want to put this point much more bluntly than I need to, because it seems to me that we often seriously misdescribe the experience of imagining other people's conditions, or of knowing what it is like to be of them, or even of having sympathy, as one of feeling and perceiving the same qualities as they do.

This seems to me wrong; that is not what it is like to know what it is like. Often one's intuitions about the condition of others do not centre on what their sensations and perceptions are but on their paralyses and energies, dynamics and tempi. These, at least in my experience, are the stuff out of which one's feel for people's moods and characters is made.

There are precedents for the situation, though we have often looked through them. Consider, for example, the phenomenal poverty of some dreams, the way in which they are more like novels, novels with the words stripped of their usual meanings and arranged in semi-transparent piles of simultaneous drafts, than they are like films. (Consider, to push the point further than many will follow me, how some dreamless sleeps differ among themselves, simply in terms of how it is different to live through them.) Then consider how important it is *how* people report their states. An avowal, whether wrung from one by circumstances or the result of introspection, is taken more as performance than as message, not because we have correlations between revealing behaviour and states of mind but because we can use the style in which confessions or complaints are made, the pattern of the language and the flow of gestures, as an object for synthesis. It is a kind of music that one can replay in imagination until one grasps the score it was played from. By seeing what it would take to act that way oneself—not what feelings or what motives, but what styles of action, what ways of tuning one's behaviour—one can fill in the gaps in what is explicitly said, to get an impression, only in part articulable, of the person's condition. One can *then* infer feelings and motives. And thus it is not essential that the starting-point be a self-ascription at all. Though, as Wittgenstein seems sometimes near to saying, some myths of the inner seem particularly suited to providing pretexts for verbal performances that tell more as performances than they do as words.

All these phenomena point to a middle level of ascription, in between the simple facts of action and the conclusions about what is thought and felt, that is often essential to knowing what someone's condition is like. Most often, one can only describe this level of ascription by means of a long list of the person's possible actions and manners, what style he would approach the world with. (Part of what it is like to be a cat is to be forever hesitating in doorways.) And then if one wants to know what this understanding can consist in if not in a sequence of thoughts, perceptions, images, and affects, I can only propose as an alternative example the form in which actions are remembered according to the model I presented, that is, as very general formulas for co-ordinating perception and muscular movement. Knowing what it is like to possess a particular mechanical skill, at any rate, may consist in knowing how someone could react suitably to any of a range of perceptions to get a desired result, and to imagine what this is like one cannot imagine all of these possible perceptions. In fact one need not imagine any of them; one just does roughly what one would do to get ready to act in the required way oneself.

IV

THE FRAGILITY OF BELIEF

THE SURFACE OF BELIEF

It is no surprise that often we cannot say in so many words what someone believes, and that we often cannot say whether someone's attitude to a proposition is belief, disbelief, or indifference. The facts seem more complex than such simple descriptions, so that even if one knew all there was to know about someone one might still be often uncertain about what beliefs to attribute. But I take this to be no radical claim; we don't expect things to be so simple. It surely isn't very awful, either, that in many such cases when we cannot say exactly what someone believes, the person's attitude to the world is not at all mysterious, one knows pretty much as well as one ever does how the person thinks things are. But it is a less evident thing, I think, that in very many of these cases in which belief is so hard to pin down one seems able to apply the same forms of explanation, in terms of what agents wanted to get and how they thought they could get what they wanted. For where are the beliefs and desires? Yet if this is not the case, if we cannot explain action in roughly the standard way even when, as is very often the case, there is no easily stated fact about someone's beliefs, then the person really is mysterious, the actions, if not the attitudes, become inexplicable.

Some hallowed forms of explanation by purpose may seem to depend on agents' having very definite sets of beliefs (and desires). These forms of explanation are not central or essential, though, as I argued in Chapter II and will argue in the next chapter. They are particular cases in a galaxy of forms of explanation, many of which do indeed turn on what an agent thinks is the case and how an agent would like things to be, but most of which apply beyond the range of cases—I actually think that they are relatively occasional—in which it is a cut-and-dried matter what the content of saying what someone believes is. The purpose of the chapter is to make this clear, and in so doing to show how fragile and specialized a notion that of belief is, how delicate its conditions of application are, and how small a role it can play in our description of people. Paradoxically, I want at the same time to bring out the strength and generality of the factors which underlie the applicability of belief; it is by usurping the position of these factors that belief can sometimes appear to have a solidity and a centrality that it does not have.

Suppose that one were trying to write down a definition of 'believes'. A believes that p if and only if . . . Lists of problem cases would arise to trouble easy definitions. I see them as falling roughly into three classes: problems about the unity of one's beliefs, problems about their objectivity, and problems about reference. For example, I wake up in the middle of the night and I tell my grumbling household, 'Shlomo has returned'. I could believe that Shlomo has returned. If I did the right things—looked for Shlomo near by, repeated my assertion in other terms, drew conclusions from it—this might be the best guess. The guess could be undermined by more information. I might refuse to unify my revelation with the rest of my beliefs, refusing in the morning to be surprised that Shlomo was not visible, or continuing to search far and wide for him. Or I disavow my assertion when I am persuaded how inconvenient it would be if Shlomo had returned. Or there is no such creature as Shlomo; or I identify Shlomo, in reality my long lost favourite cat, with my pillow. Depending on the details, we might redescribe my state as something other than belief, as conjecture, fantasy, free-association, confusion. The facts that support an initial attribution of belief may be extended rather than denied; belief is then excluded, but yet more facts could make the state be describable again as belief, and so on. One can begin to see how a form of explanation that applies to beliefs will most likely be of more general application, and how it may well *have* to be of more general application if it is to make any connections

out its rivals and letting the resulting commitment guide one's research.

Either of these strategies may be rational or both may be. Both react to the destruction of the former disconnectedness of one's beliefs by instituting a new disconnection, between what is believed and what is rejected or half-believed. The first strategy results in few beliefs and a larger number of quasi-beliefs, and the second results in more beliefs and fewer quasi-beliefs (since the price paid for belief in these circumstances is the loss of any affirmative attitude to the propositions that have turned out to be incompatible with what is believed). Crudely put, the first strategy is most likely to be rational when there is a practical matter at hand to be dealt with, and one has chosen or been chosen as the person to deal with it. For example, one believes in an astronomical scheme (central sun and crystal spheres, say) that has just been shown to conflict with other beliefs and with observation; one has to have a model of the heavens in order to navigate the oceans and pick auspicious days for love and enterprise. Clearly one should go on using the discredited scheme, expressing one's doubts and hoping for something better. And the second strategy is most likely to be rational when it is a matter of theoretical concern, and there are others around who will defend the beliefs that one rather arbitrarily abandons. Thus, different schools or styles of set theory hold on to different selections from Frege's inconsistent axioms, developing and expanding them until eventually, we all hope, it will become clearer which course is the right one.

The two strategies can clearly be combined. One can also, if one is very subtle, follow a third strategy. One maintains hold of all the threatened beliefs, as in the first strategy, and holds them with a force approaching belief, as in the second strategy, but avoids the contradiction one knows is lying in wait by carefully staying off the path that leads to it. One looks ahead and avoids, so far as one can, any situation in which possibly conflicting propositions will be considered together. Very tricky, very dangerous, and like the first strategy it results in attitudes of conjecture, inclination, assurance, even insistence—sometimes rationally so—but not of belief. Paradoxically perhaps, in this state and in that which results from the first strategy, one's actions are much as they were before the discovery of the contradiction, though one has few of the same beliefs (in the relevant area). Paradoxically, too, the stupider or more irrational one is, the more one's attitude is like belief, for the less does one's thought negotiate the now delicate path between the conflicting propositions. The more aware one is of the conflict the more one sees the tension between acting as one wants and having beliefs that can be true, and the harder it is to describe one's state as that of belief. Attitudes do not fail to be belief just by being separated from the main body of belief; they fail to be belief when they are *held* separate.

PARTISANSHIP: SUSCEPTIBILITY TO DESIRE

Everyone knows that widgets have no wedges; it is taught in schools and recorded in encyclopedias. Until one day Brasnicus, a demented sage, gives in a public lecture excellent reasons why widgets have to have wedges, forty-nine apiece. Brasnicus doesn't *believe* this; it is a matter of public debate whether old Brasnicus believes anything at all. One student mostly sleeping in the audience hears without knowing he hears, and years later when he is eminent and respectable conjectures, in a widely discussed and little respected article, that widgets have wedges. *He* does not believe it, mind you, but he conjectures it, he thinks that there is something in the idea and one ought to find out how much. The scientific world divides into wedgeites and anti-wedgeites, all furiously experimenting and deducing final refutation of the blockheads on the other side. The opposed movements become associated with different ethics and politics, and a grand crisis of the culture seems to be looming when a young scholar called Zweistein rediscovers Brasnicus's arguments and settles the issue.

At what stage in the process are beliefs acquired? It depends on the nature of the debate. Many cooler intellects may have been able to work with their conjectures, hunches, and commitments without treating them as beliefs, until Zweistein came along and gave proper grounds for belief; others, less temperate and perhaps less rational, may have been unable to work towards establishing their favoured hypotheses without taking it as a fact that it was true, the only problem being that of convincing the other side. At any rate, in the development from conjecture to knowledge belief *need* not enter until the very end. (And when we consider not the beliefs of individuals but community-wide belief, acceptance as doctrine, it is clear how many variations and gradations there are between an individual's brave conjecture and the community's belief.)

Compare two research teams, one devoted to getting a result that will refute the faith of the other, and the other devoted to showing that the result cannot be got, perhaps by establishing an opposite result. Neither bunch has evidence that the other has not, ignoring the small delay required for scientific gossip, spies, and preliminary reports to communicate each team's goings-on to the other. Each is composed of perfectly sensible people. And yet each is firmly committed to something the other is just as firmly opposed to, may in fact regard as absurd. Neither need take the other as composed of fools, for each can recognize the origin of its different convictions in the inevitable force of scientific partisanship. A fresh Ph.D., before being recruited for either team, may have no tenderness for either's hypothesis, but after joining a team he comes soon enough to share its hopes of success. If recruits didn't or couldn't they would be unable to perform as members of the team.

Scientific partisans have their convictions, or whatever you want to call them, as a result of wanting a conjecture to turn out to be true, or a line of research to pay off, or an intellectual tradition to be vindicated. Their desires influence their convictions. This is as it should be; they would not push themselves hard enough if moved by bare impartial curiosity: fewer truths would be discovered. And it is not just in the context of partisanship that one's desires ought to influence one's convictions. Imagine someone analysing a chemical compound. The point at which he declares that it has a certain constitution—the variety of tests he puts it to, and the definiteness he requires of the results of these tests—will be different in the two cases in which it is merely a matter of the success of a class-room demonstration and in the case in which lives depend on it (if it were, say, a sample of a new vaccine which would be fatal if contaminated). One's desires certainly also influence the conjectures one makes; one investigates possibilities connected with what one would like to be true. The intensive investigation of possible cancer-producing viruses in the past few years is clearly based as much on the hope that if such viruses exist we might be able to find vaccines against them as it is on the evidence, not originally or even now all that strong, that viruses play much of a role in human cancer.

There is a difference between believing something as a result of having certain desires and having a belief that is *based on* desires. The beliefs that result from the practice of science are inevitably shaped by the fact that scientists have motives, loyalties, aspirations. In claiming to believe something, though, one is asserting that the world actually is as one thinks, and then any justification one gives will have to be independent of one's motivation. Though one may admit that one believes because of what one wants, one must also claim that those wants could change leaving that belief still in place. Otherwise, belief becomes fantasy, wishful thinking.[1]

The situation is different for conjectures, hypotheses, fighting claims, hopeful stabs in the dark. One can quite reasonably say: here's my guess, and I wouldn't guess it if I didn't want p to be true, or x discomfited. Of course, the closer their connection with their motivation, the less support such states can give to beliefs, real beliefs. The rational person has another delicate

[1] The quarrel between Hume and Descartes about whether desires can (should, may) shape beliefs has got connected in more recent times to many other questions. See William James's discussion in the title essay of *The Will to Believe and other essays* (Longmans Green, London, 1897), Chapter 9, and the appendix of Jurgen Habermas, *Knowledge and Human Interests* (Beacon Press, Boston, 1971), and H. H. Price, 'Belief and Will', *Proc. Arist. Soc. Supplementary* Vol. 28, 1954, pp. 1–26. I suspect that in the more recent discussions the differences are really about the extension of belief, and that none of the participants doubt that some belief-like states are and should be influenced by wants and that something like my innocuous formulation in the text above is correct.

balance to bring off: one has to keep one's beliefs insulated, at least a little bit insulated, from all these other states, lest their saturation with desire seep into the beliefs. Clearly here, too, only the very wise keep such distinctions operating in their thinking and doing; only the wise, in our culture, worry, or need to worry, how much they believe of what they think.[2]

REFERENCE: ARTICULABILITY

The object of this section is a particular kind of orphanage that can befall a belief. Too simply put, a belief requires the union ot a syntactic and a semantic component; a grammatical sentence expresses what a belief says about certain objects or properties. And when one of these two is missing a state that would otherwise be a perfectly normal belief is isolated from its normal functioning.

A remark of Wittgenstein introduces one of the least controversial class of such cases. 'Someone says "Napoleon was crowned in 1804". I ask him "Did you mean the man who won the battle of Austerlitz?" He says "Yes, I meant him".—Does

---

[2] It is not only in scientific contexts that these issues arise. They are clearly found in questions about self-deception. Typically, this involves the deformation of a person's convictions under the influence of desires or commitments. People are constrained to think well of themselves and those they love, and so when faced with evidence of vice (inadequacy, treason) they do their best to explain it away. This much is *not* folly; at any rate it is a clear consequence of commitment and is as reasonable as scientific partisanship. It becomes perverse when the evidence mounts to a point where it can no longer be denied just via one's commitment to see the evidence in a certain light, with a certain aim. Even then, people's refusal to grant the obvious may just establish them as foolish, blindly stubborn. But in typical cases of self-deception something stranger happens. The person at the same time maintains the affirmation and admits the force of the evidence against it, with a shrug of the shoulders at the discrepancy. Recent writers on self-deception have worried whether one's attitude to the proposition ought then to be called belief. The facts about the person do not seem extraordinarily unclear, though, and inasmuch as they do not determine whether the situation is one of belief the trouble lies as much with the concept of belief as with the self-deceived person's tangled thinking. The tangles are there, and it's an interesting thing that we can get into them, and an important thing that we *have* to get near to them in order to be faithful friends and self-respecting people, but the nature of the tangle is not clarified by taking what we understand about it and on the basis of this asking: Is it belief?

this mean that when he "meant him" he in some way thought of Napoleon's winning the battle of Austerlitz?' Of course it does not; one's use of a name is not tied to any of the descriptions one believes to apply to its bearer. Something similar is true even if there is no name involved.[3] Someone learns first that there was a man born in Corsica in 1769 who went on to various exploits; as he learns more about the man he just thinks '*he* did that' without identifying *him* particularly as the man crowned in 1804 or the victor of Austerlitz or whatever. Then if the story gets mixed up—say, he assimilates Louis and Napoleon Bonaparte and comes to believe that the victor of Austerlitz is the king of Holland in 1806 and the father of Napoleon III, then there may be no fact to the matter about who his beliefs refer to. What does he believe then? Not just that Napoleon became king of Holland in 1806, but that *he* was, where *he* is a creature of his private mythology, linked with both Napoleon and Louis Bonaparte. There is not, at any rate there need not be, any way of capturing his belief by saying that he believes that *p*, where *p* is some real proposition, seducible into English.

If someone's beliefs are very much out of touch with reality, as we who are describing the beliefs construe it, then this sort of thing may be ubiquitous. We may feel more or less secure in describing many of his states as states of belief and have some rough grasp of their content, and yet be unable to state them in our sentences. A basic reason for our security in calling what he has beliefs is likely to be the presence of familiar syntactical forms in his assertions and by inference in his thought. He believes that *x* was king of Holland in 1806, and the only problem, which may be insoluble, is in finding the right word for *x*. With sufficient ingenuity in characterizing the person's mythology we may succeed in getting a description of roughly what he believes, even if we cannot pin down his beliefs one by one.

---

[3] Ludwig Wittgenstein, *The Blue and Brown Books* (Harper and Row, New York, 1958), p. 39. It is clear that these issues are connected with issues of the relation between names and descriptions discussed by Russell, Searle, and Kripke, and also clear that the issues are not quite the same.

The concept of belief is clearly beginning to feel some strain here, even it does not break.

Real breakage of the concept occurs when there is not enough of a syntactical form to compensate for the failings of the referential component. Consider for example perceptual beliefs. One sees a cat and sees it where it is and believes that *it* is *there*. We identify such a belief by referring to the elements of the fact it represents. We put it into words by ascribing to one the belief that the object one is perceiving, as described by its perceptual relation to one ('the cat in my line of sight five feet away') has whatever properties we take one to perceive it to have. This strategy does not work when the object does not exist or is not related to the believer in the right way, for example, in hallucinations. If I have a hallucinatory impression just like the state I would have if the cat were before me then my belief that there is a cat before me is unproblematic, just as it is when I see the cat, for it has a syntactical medium quite independent of its failed reference. But what about the state of mind that corresponds to the perceptual belief that *that* cat is *there*? I am still in that state, but, since the syntax isn't intrinsic to it and since the referential element is absent—and the apparent syntax of the sentence embedded in the ascription of belief was just a way of tracing the state's reference to that cat, now absent, and its occupation of that location, perhaps now imaginary—we find ourselves unable to call it a belief. We can still say roughly what state it is; what it is like to be in it; we say 'it's like believing of a cat that it is before one' or 'it is like the state of belief from which one would have inferred that there is a cat before one if there really had been one there'.

An opposite orphanage occurs when although the state in question does refer, is appropriately hooked up to, particular objects, the syntactical element is inadequate. The syntactical form we assign a belief serves three functions; it indicates the kinds of things the belief is about, it indicates the form of words the believer might use to express the belief, and it indicates the role the belief plays in the believer's thinking. With beliefs of a fairly explicit sort the last two of these amount to much the same thing. But as we push the concept of belief beyond that of the easily expressed and explicitly asserted, verbal expression and cognitive role begin to come apart. It is important, though, that the concept of belief include regions like this, where it is clearer what a belief is about than what form of words best expresses it. For the ability to ascribe such remote beliefs is one of the psychological richnesses of our science and our culture. Classical epistemology allows us to describe people's judgements of appearance; it allows us to say how people believe things look and feel. Freud shows us how to ascribe to people beliefs clothed in the 'language' of primal fantasy.

There is not going to be any once-and-for-all deduction of the variety of conceptualization we can profitably build into the beliefs we ascribe to people, if only because the extent of this variety depends on facts, about the structure of our thought and about the limits of our attributive capacities, that are not going to reveal themselves *a priori*. Since we are, roughly and given a lot of philosophical disagreement over the details, all aware of this, we do not expect that the variety of beliefs a person can have need correspond exactly to the variety of linguistic resources we or that person happens to have available. And this leaves us open to all sorts of complications.

The easiest hard cases are those in which someone uses a language with different expressive powers to that in which one is describing his beliefs. One doesn't have words for everything he asserts, but one has reason to believe that everything is linguistically in order, that he is using the language correctly and there are no failures of reference. Then, as in the parallel cases in which syntax was unproblematic and reference was confused, we find little difficulty in saying that the person has beliefs and is expressing them; we just cannot list them one by one. But, inevitably, as the syntactical clothing of the state becomes more and more remote from any explicitly linguistic form, we get nearer and nearer to the point at which we cannot describe the person's states as beliefs at all. Intermediate cases are those in which the person's use of the syntax, whether or not it is the same as that in which the belief is being reported, is

flawed, to the point not just of solecism but of real uncertainty
about the intelligibility of what is presented. When Hegel says
'The Idea ... imparts ... to universality the right to prove itself,
not only the ground and necessary form of particularity, but
also . . . its final end', we know, roughly, what he is talking
about, but we are so uncertain what he is saying about it that
we are in real doubt whether there is a belief that is being
expressed. Yet we have no doubt that there is some state of
mind that formed around those words, which may, for all we
know, be just the right words to express it; it just may not be
belief. Extreme cases are those in which the appropriate
reference exists in the absence of all syntax. Here our refusal to
ascribe a belief, though we know what properties and objects
are being spoken of, extends to scepticism that there is any state
at all, of which the words uttered can properly be taken to be
an expression.

It is easy to see why we do not restrict our attributions of
belief to cases in which it is perfectly clear what objects are
being referred to, or to cases in which the words we use to
describe the belief are those the believer says or thinks them.
There are so few such cases, and if one of the two elements,
syntax or reference, is unproblematic, then we need not require
perfection of the other in order for the attribution of belief to
serve its usual purposes. Given that this is the way we use the
concept, though, it is inevitable that the cases in which reference
and syntax are jointly strong enough to support the attribution
of belief are surrounded by a penumbra of other cases which are
like cases of belief in many significant respects but in which the
application of the concept of belief must be doubtful, metaphorical, or impossible.

THE DIMENSIONS

These have been ordinary hard cases. Ordinary because they
are of kinds that occur all the time, and are not inherently
mysterious, and hard because they cause trouble when one tries
to spell out the content of the claim that someone believes
something. In discussing them I tried to bring out how our

understanding of them depends on our evaluating the state of the person in question in terms of various concepts rather more primitive than that of belief. The relations between a belief-like state and an agent's motivation, its referential relations to the environment, the words with which it might be expressed, and the reasoning that connects it with other such states, are often perfectly clear, when it seems merely academic, perversely philosophical, to find it important whether the state is one of belief. Call these concepts *objectivity, reference, unity, syntacti- cality*. The terms are not particularly apt, and I would not claim that these are the really fundamental concepts or that they are comprehensive enough. But they do suffice for a clumsy classification of the cases we have considered. If we lay out an axis for each of the four elements we have considered, and let the distance from the origin along any axis represent the extent to which that element is *absent* (so that, for example, the further along the objectivity axis one goes the less objectivity is being ascribed) we get the following diagram. I have marked in crude names for typical kinds of state of not-quite belief, and marked in a (four-dimensional) half-star-shaped region at the centre that represents the range of states falling under the concept of belief.

To be a belief, a state must be near the centre of the graph; it must have all these elements to a fairly high degree, subject to a not at all trivial complication I discuss in the next section. Notice, however, that the greater any one element is (the nearer the point representing the state is to some axis) the less the need for the other elements to be great. The reason for this is that each of these components contributes to a particular effect, which is at the core of the concept of belief, so that a sufficiency of one of them can compensate for a deficiency of another. The clearer the referential component of a belief, for example in normal perceptual beliefs, the less need is there for it to have an explicit syntactical clothing, for one knows what it is about and what it attributes to what it is about. Similarly, the more explicit the syntax, the less dependence there is on successful reference, for, again, one knows what is being said, the content has a

THE DIMENSIONS OF BELIEF

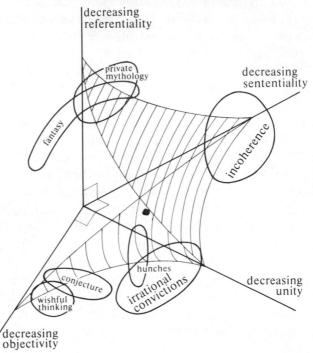

Representation of belief-like states in a four-dimensioned schematism. The area within the half-star-shaped shaded boundary corresponds to states that can be expressed with 'believes'. Note that the terms for belief-like states (conjectures, fantasies, convictions) typically include states both describable and not describable as belief.

medium, though it is not the things themselves. Taking a different pair of axes, it is clear that the more a state is unified with the body of one's other beliefs, the less does it matter to its characterization as a belief that it lacks objectivity, that it depends for its position in one's thought on its relation to one's wishes. Conversely, the more objective, the freer from the taint of wishful thinking, a belief is, the less its being a belief depends on its integration with what else one believes. For in either case one has suitable material for inference; one can get to and from the belief largely by reasoning alone.

It is clear enough what underlies these compensations. The invariant of each is something that is required in order for the states in question to form parts of a greater pattern of belief, depicting in its various parts ways that parts of reality may be. Beliefs are pieces in a jig-saw puzzle, each region of which has to make a claim on the world. So an isolated piece can yet be a belief if it is of a sort that could be connected with the main pattern. The shapes by virtue of which the pieces hook to one another are their syntax, the colours on them are their pretensions to reference. So a piece can have little colour if it serves to hold others together, and can have few hooks or cavities if it is a sufficiently accurate depiction of some real corner of the world that its place with respect to other pieces describing nearby regions can be determined.

We construe states as organized into larger patterns of belief in order to be able to trace paths through them. That is, many of the ways in which we explain and imagine action require us to trace a sequence of states and actions which follow an objective, reconstructible sequence from beginning to end. One wants to be able to assume an initial state and then relate it to a later state not by idiosyncratic laws of association but by the fact that both states are parallel reflections of the facts. In particular, one wants to be able to relate beliefs to the conditions in the world that evoke and result from them, and to be able to describe the evolution of beliefs and desires into others which bear some logical relation to them. Three aspects of belief are thus essentially tied together: the unity of beliefs in coherent systems, their quality of representing the world, and their expression in sentences (sometimes via the grammatical presentation of belief as a verb governing an embedded sentence).

What lies behind each of these aspects of belief is the fact that we want at the same time to take beliefs as relations agents have to their environment and as termini of chains of reasoning. Thus the appeal of representing a belief as an attitude to a proposition; the embedded sentence which presents the believed proposition both refers to the objects named and described in it and is suited to be part of chains of argument. Thus some of the difficulties of the concept too, since the two functions do not always coincide perfectly, as when perception makes one believe something in contradiction to one's system of belief, or when one's beliefs are seriously false, purporting to represent things which do not exist.

It is as if we laid a web about those things in the world that are objects of our interest, and followed the lines of this web about, going from one node of it to another when we reason and from the web to the objects it adheres to when we perceive or act. This metaphor is made into an explicit theory in the appendix to this chapter. Putting a detailed exposition of the idea aside until then, let us see the function of the dual nature of ascriptions of belief in psychological explanation. Consider two kinds of explanatory principles.

First we have principles that say what can be expected of a particular person or of the effects of a particular kind of mood or personality. 'If he thinks someone has worked against him, he'll never forget, but wait and eventually cause harm in return', 'she was in that state of wild hopefulness in which one takes even the faintest signs of success as unambiguous portents'. I think we pick up these principles as we find them: one by one, as an unordered variety of useful guides, sometimes making them up on the spot. What is general and systematic in these principles is the use they make of the concept of belief. The simplest of them suppose the agent to be situated in a particular way with respect to particular objects in his environment (as typically indicated by wide-scope quantifiers and a *de re* tonality to the intensional idioms) and then describe the course he follows around them. More subtle principles situate the agent with respect to the structure of his own beliefs, touching the environment only 'around the edges', and describe his dance across that not particularly well-defined stage. Clearly in the transition from the simpler to the subtler principles progressively less reliance is placed on reference via perception and the possibility of action, and more on the syntactical connections of beliefs, and on the role of these connections in mediating reference. The common source of generality, as I termed it in Chapter II, which provides the conformity of diverse principles of this kind to a common explanatory style, is provided by a particular understanding of the referential and inferential connections of beliefs, to which the various belief-like concepts used in the style have to conform. If you want to know more, read the appendix.

The second kind of explanatory principle is that of general motivational schemata, ways in which we take desires to result in action. I discuss these at some length in the next chapter; the only points to make here are that in both the practical reasoning by which desire leads to intention and the energizing process by which intention and desire spark action, the tendency of desire is to lead away from the fixed and intelligible, given by reference and inference: it has little respect for either. And thus the function of belief, in the interests of making action intelligible, is to tie down the states of mind one appeals to, via reference to the world and via inference to each other.

No doubt the subtle exact sense of the ascription of a belief, or a hunch, a conjecture, an expectation, a fantasy, matters to the appropriateness of particular explanatory principles. The work is done by the underlying dimensions though; it is the reference, the sententiality, the objectivity (and whatever other dimensions there may be) of a state of mind that allow it to serve the function of a belief. And for these to serve their function it does not make much difference whether these factors are present in exactly the right proportions, and other disturbing factors sufficiently absent, for some idiomatic or philosophical connotation of 'belief' to apply. What does matter is whether the amounts and proportions and relations of these factors will serve the function of belief, of providing a map through which to follow the agent's thought and action. If they will, then with properly confident disregard of the niceties of the language, we apply any principle we can.

FITTING CONDITIONS

From what I have said so far it would seem that the possession of a belief (or of some belief-like state) is marked by the simultaneous presence of various quite distinct elements, which by their coincidence make belief. If this were so, then the grammatical forms we use to ascribe beliefs, would convey a misleading impression of the unity of the state. It would be better to say something like: a believes, of $o_1, o_2, \ldots, o_n$, that they satisfy the sentential form $p[o_1, o_2, \ldots, o_n]$, thus keeping the force of the belief, its reference, and its sentential components quite separate. And some recent suggestions about the logical form of belief-sentences do amount to this. Things are not this simple, though; the representation of belief as a propositional attitude has more to commend it than just that it brings together the various components of belief. There has to be a kind of unity to these components, and I must now discuss it.

The basic observation is that to make a belief there has to be a kind of congruence between the various factors involved. For example a belief expressed in articulately verbal terms cannot obtain its reference simply as a result of perception, as a purely perceptual belief can. If I believe that the father of Paleface and Wonton is now overturning the garbage can, then it is not enough for my belief to be about the cat at the moment getting into trouble that I see him at it; I have to connect what I see with an identification of him as the perpetrator of the earlier crime that resulted in the kittens.

When a belief refers to a particular object, when it is about that object in particular, there is a definite relation, usually involving a causal chain between the object and the possession of the belief. But what relations will support reference in this way depends on what kind of a belief it is. A similar thing happens with the sentential content of a belief; the relation between the sentence one uses to characterize it and the nature of the state itself is not a constant one. For some kinds of belief it is a misrepresentation not to give as the content just about exactly the words the person would use to express it (ignoring complications about paraphrase and translation), while with others the only way to specify the content is to extract a sentence from the causes, references, or inferential connections of the belief.

The source of these complications is the variety of states and subject-matters that we permit under the name of belief. In each case we want there to be a claim to reference, and if possible successful reference, and in each case we want there to be a sentence whose logical relations are similar to the inferential relations of the belief in the agent's thought. And we want these to go together, the same believed proposition both to name the object of belief and to pick out the logical connections. But what we have to do to pull off this trick, the way we have to construe reference and sentential content, varies according to what as a matter of fact are a belief's causal connections with the environment and inferential relations with other states. We react to this situation by taking the image of the web of belief seriously, and when picking the words to describe a belief we try to locate the belief, with respect to other beliefs and the environment. If we have to, we abandon the easy 'believe that p' idiom and describe reference, unity, and so on separately, trying also to show how they all come together.

As a result there are persistent ambiguities when a sufficiently subtle context or a sufficiently borderline belief creates uncertainty about which region of belief is in question. Consider two examples. First, the Confused Detective: one says of him that 'he has an opinion about who did it; he thinks that it was the Orange Lipstick murderer again, but he doesn't have any idea who *that* is. I fear that he is beginning to suspect his own staff, in fact he's pretty sure that someone known to him is the lipstick killer, but he doesn't yet know who.' Here the use of different 'who' idioms, whose function is to indicate that there is an object to which the object refers, is in a delicate disaccord. On the one hand he believes of someone, the Orange Lipstick murderer in fact, that he did it, and on the other hand since he hasn't come to any conclusion which of several people is the lipstick killer, he *doesn't* believe of that one of them who is the culprit that he did it. There is quite evidently no real contradiction here. There are two referential relations being indicated; the detective believes of the killer with respect to the one, and not with respect to the other, that he did it. The first relation takes the belief 'the Orange Lipstick murderer did it' as belief in the context of files of past crimes and descriptions of criminal styles, the criminologist's web around the facts; the second relation takes it in the context of physical apprehension of someone among those available to be apprehended, caught up in the practical policeman's more carnivorous net.

Second, a description of Henry James's attitude to his approaching fifth birthday party: 'Henry's expectations on the matter were, I thought, marked by a very definite avoidance of the explicit and, though these are not the words he would have used, by a not too inconsiderable tendency to refer to an unspecified something which, if it appeared too clearly as something he could grasp as a *so* and be sure that however fine and pleasant it might be it was not one of those others he hardly dared name or hope for, would bring him to regard it with hardly disguised distaste, as not at all the event he had so carefully described to himself.' Here the intentional avoidance of anything Henry might actually say serves to attribute to his five-year-old state of mind all the subtlety of the inferential connections surrounding the sentence that gives the content of his belief. Was *that* really the content of what he thought? Yes, according to one relation of content to state, and No, according to another: this elaborate sentence gives a good representation of a maze of thoughts in little Henry's head, and it does not give any idea of what he might say or agree to.

We may despair of understanding the connections between beliefs, their objects, and their contents, if we see just this maze of relations, varying according to the type of belief. But there has to be an order underneath the whole mess, even if it is difficult to find the right terms to express it. There has to be an over-all unity to a person's beliefs; they have to form some sort of system. Inferences from one kind of belief to another have to make sense; reference to objects and properties has to be transmitted through the boundaries between different kinds of belief.

Though all the pieces, all the kinds of state that can be called belief, have to fit together, somehow, the variety of pieces and fittings may be limitless. Any formulation of the over-all coherence will have to be pretty abstract. Apart from what I say in the appendix I have no such formulation to offer. To get one, what seems to be required is a combination of solutions to two long-unsolved problems. If we had a general criterion of knowledge, or if we had a working theory of reference, then we could give a general definition of belief. (If we could make oil from water, we could all have enough to eat.) What I mean is this: one central issue in the complicated debate about which any set of necessary and sufficient conditions properly catches the concept of knowledge concerns the formulation of evidential connections between known items. What we know depends on perception in some respects, on memory from beliefs acquired in childhood in others, and so on. Philosophers such as Alvin Goldman and Gilbert Harman are engaged in extracting from the analysis of examples, cognitive psychology, and anything else that seems useful, general formulations of these evidential connections that tie perceptual beliefs, theoretical beliefs, mathematical beliefs, and even perhaps moral beliefs, into a common system of knowledge attributable to an epistemic agent. To the extent that their attempts succeed, the connections that get drawn between different kinds of belief hold for beliefs that are not knowledge too, and thus 'solve' one part of our problem. The other part of it would be solved if we could say how a term occurring in the particular use of a particular sentence comes, via an inconceivable variety of detours through beliefs, perceptual relations, tellings of stories, and recordings in cultural objects such as books, to refer to a particular object. If we could state this in any generality then, since beliefs form one possible link in referential chains, a definition of what it was for a belief to refer to an object would drop out.[4]

---

[4] For analyses of knowledge of the kind I am discussing see Alvin Goldman, 'A Causal Theory of Knowing', *Journal of Philosophy* 64, 1967, 'Innate Knowledge', in S. P. Stich, ed., *Innate Ideas* (University of California Press, Berkeley, 1975), 'Epistemics', *Journal of Philosophy* 75, 1978, Gilbert Harman, *Thought* (Princeton U.P., 1973). For analyses of reference see Saul Kripke, *Naming and Necessity* in D. Davidson and G. Harman, eds., *Semantics of Natural Languages* (Reidel, Dordrecht, 1971), and Hilary Putnam, 'Meaning and Reference', *Journal of Philosophy* 70, 1973.

Now I do not expect that either of these problems will be settled soon. And, while they are important problems in their own right, I do not think that it matters much for the understanding of belief that they are not solved. For what is essential to the concept of belief is that it unites references to objects and inferential connections into a network within which we manage to trace patterns which explain agents' actions. It would be interesting to know how this uniting is done, and thus to understand what range of psychological states can qualify as beliefs. But without knowing it we can see what the elements that are thus united are, and see how great the variety of ways in which they can be united is.

THE MYTH OF BELIEF

There could be beings who normally represented their environment in terms that were not at all affected by their desires, transparent in their conceptualization, congruent with their speech, who had states whose only function was to represent what was around them. One can imagine such creatures most easily at two extremes: uncomplicated and wordless but not altogether stupid beasts, and perfect dispassionate philosophers; simple perceivers and epistemological marvels. As for the rest of us, we're somewhere in between. Our attempts at uncomplicated perception are compromised by our persistently complicated cognition, and our attempts at detached rationality are fouled by our persistently human motivation. Evidently this is not to say that we do not have beliefs, but that our possession of them is tempered by our imperfections, and that our attributions of them take these imperfections into account. We do this, I think, by the enormous subtlety of our modes of attribution, and by the imposition upon ourselves of a myth about our natures.

Wittgenstein remarked that believing is, in some ways, for some purposes, better classed with fearing and hoping than it is with thinking and concluding.[5] The long list of roughly affirmative states, of believing, hoping, thinking, conjecturing . . . is

[5] *Philosophical Investigations* (Macmillan, New York, 1953), p. 574.

arranged, we arrange it, so that we can say what we want of people. If we use 'believes' as a member of the list, with self-conscious contrast to the others, we tend to mean not what occurs to one or what one thinks but what one holds to and publicly asserts, one's credo. One can repeat it in the face of threatening evidence; presumably this is what Wittgenstein has in mind. We also use 'believes' as a particularly neutral member of the list. We say what one believes—we use 'thinks' this way too—and surround our saying this with descriptions of how one is situated with respect to the objects of one's belief, the terms one uses to oneself and in public expression, and how one will be led to act on it, so that when all is said and done it is clear, clear enough, where one's state is on the grid of the dimensions of belief, and how reference and content are to be taken.

And so if we take it in this way 'believes' does not really have an extension. Whenever we say what one believes we are ascribing something to one (describing one as being in a certain state, of its being a definite way between one and the world). So are we when we say that one conjectures or hopes or is inclined to think something. But the states that are ascribed to people when we say these things need not divide up into states of belief and states of conjecture and so on. For the function of labelling someone's state 'belief', 'conjecture' or whatever, is usually not to describe, just by using that tag, what kind of state it is, but to get a start on putting together a mass of information about the person, to arrive at a representation of the way they are. And thus we could just drop the verb 'to believe', and get along perfectly well, saying just the same things about people, in a few more words. Of course, if we dropped the whole list, of 'believes' 'thinks', 'suspects', . . ., we'd be in trouble; but no one of them is essential.

Even seen this way, though, some connotations of a more particular sense of belief emerge, in which belief is neither just one of a list of representational states nor a neutral core for an accretion of further specifications. Belief is still attached to public affirmation, to the results of sage deliberations, and to what we gather from observation. These points of congealment are convenient for its use as a neutral beginning for further specification, for they are three obvious vertices of an epistemological pattern that all the states in this continuum are, with varying degrees of tightness, shaped around. Whatever else they are, they are all attempts at representing the world around their possessor, and so they all must pay some respect to its more obvious nudgings, though that respect may take the form of grudging acknowledgement or defiance. And they must all have some ambition to find a place in one's final considered sworn-to description of things, though this ambition may be unrealized and this final summing-up never achieved. It is not to push the matter too much further, then, or perhaps it is to push it considerably further from an opening point that is a clear invitation to the attempt, to tell a story, invent a myth, about a state of mind called belief, which has *only* those properties needed to make it respond to evidence and result in opinion. It is nothing but a naked candidate for knowledge.

We do sometimes explain our actions in accordance with this myth, stringing out long chains of hypothetical inferences and assuming a miraculous dispassionate measured rationality. The rationality by itself may not be inappropriate; some people under some circumstances do show a lot of it. What is unlikely is the supposition that a person's rationality takes the form of representational states that are quite unseducible by desire and articulated in perfect harmony with their speech. It is unlikely just because we have no reason to believe that people possess such states, and no presupposition of their existence is involved just in our use of the concept of belief. That concept presupposes only the underlying dimensions; it certainly does not presuppose any limits to our rationality, but it leaves quite open by what combinations of states we achieve it.

There is no denying, though, that something like the myth as I have described it does play an important role in our culture. We take it as a source of easily explainable patterns of actions and, with these patterns in mind as sketched out by epistemologists and economists and decision theorists, we act in accordance with them when we want our actions to be particularly intelligible and the beliefs and desires they stem from particularly easily read. Mind you, the explanations we get thereby are not nearly as innocent as they seem, for the real factors that lead someone to act in accordance with the patterns they adduce are vastly more complicated and culture-bound than they insinuate. In any case, this myth and this regulative ideal of behaviour are not to be taken as tied to the concept of belief but as one of the possibilities that the concept, as defined in its 'universal' form by the system of dimensions and the web that unites them, allows.

What this brings out most vividly is, I think, how little common sense constrains the real nature of the psychological states it alludes to. Common sense does not require that there be any particular determinate kind of states called 'beliefs'. The best psychological theory might not provide us with the means for picking out any such natural kind. It might be that the basic currency of mental life is that of primal fantasies *a la* Freud or Klein or of items of stored non-asserted, non-propositional information, as in some theories of memory, leaving, perhaps, no room for beliefs. Or the opposite could turn out to be the case. The best theory could hold that conjectures, hopes, thoughts, fantasies, memories, are all explainable in terms of something like belief. For instance, a theory of various degrees of belief, much like the theory of subjective probability, might prove capable of explaining all the ways we represent things. But of course it's far too early to make a philosopher's judgement on these matters; none of these theories may prove basic enough.

We may not see how little the true facts are constrained if we let a misleading picture guide our intuitions. It is to think of mental life as a stream of conscious thoughts, each of which bears assertive force. There are one's occurrent thoughts, and the rest of one's beliefs consist in the stock of thoughts that could be summoned to this forum and said Yes to. The picture is all wrong; in assimilating to mental assent all the forms of assertive attitude that there can be, and in assimilating to the conscious presence of a sentence the variety of ways in which content may be determined. It not only misleads us about what may actually be going on when we have beliefs, thoughts, conjectures, but it presents a totally misleading picture of what it is like to be a thinking agent.[6]

---

[6] Though many ideas behind this chapter are taken from other writers, I do not find it easy to identify the things I say here as taken from this or that writer and acknowledge them as I use them. I am generally indebted to David Armstrong's eclectic attitude in *Belief, Truth, and Knowledge* (C.U.P., 1973), and to Richard Jeffrey, *The Logic of Decision* (McGraw-Hill, New York, 1967). Reading Hempel, Popper, and Kuhn has cured me of seeing the acceptance of hypotheses as resulting from a simple digesting of evidence, and thus from seeing belief as the central attribute of the scientist.

APPENDIX TO CHAPTER IV:
NETWORK SEMANTICS FOR BELIEF

The aim of this appendix is to give a formal treatment of the concept of belief, with two aims in mind. First, I want to provide a framework in which the enormous variety of idioms of belief acquires some unity, without diminishing the importance of the differences between them. One can believe that Leslie loves Robin, believe of Leslie and Robin that they are lovers, believe that someone loves Robin, believe Leslie to be loved by Robin. All of these are different and can serve to express different facts, but all are expressions of the same concept of belief.[1] My other aim is to present an account of how the semantically characteristic features of belief, notably its intensionality and its standard expression as a propositional attitude, arise out of its function in psychological explanation. The two aims are connected; my analysis of the second constrains belief to be a second-order concept—it involves properties of properties and quantification over properties—and it is in terms of this second-order analysis that I formulate the common and varying content of all these idioms.

THE ORIGIN OF INTENSIONALITY

I think that to describe actions in the way we do is to commit ourselves to explaining them in terms of intensional attitudes of agents (for example by their beliefs, desires, intentions). To simplify the argument, I take the relation between explanatory hypothesis and explained event to be one of deduction.

---

[1] This project is often expressed as an attempt to reconcile idioms of belief that seem to be extensional with those that are intensional. See W. V. Quine, 'Quantifiers and Propositional Attitudes', *Journal of Philosophy* 53, 1956, pp. 177–87; David Kaplan, 'Quantifying In' in *Words and Objections*, ed. Davidson and Hintikka (Reidel, Dordrecht, 1969); John Wallace, 'Belief and Satisfaction', *Nous* 6, 1972, pp. 85–95; and my 'Because He Thought He Had Insulted Him', *Journal of Philosophy* 72, 1975, pp. 5–15.

Actions consist primarily in changes in the world brought about by agents. Where a is an agent and e an event, 'e was brought about by a' can make sense for almost any e. And besides idioms like 'brought about', 'made it be that', 'is responsible for', which convert descriptions of events, and sometimes of facts, into ascriptions of agency, we can describe just about any sequence of events connected by the actions of a human agent by use of the standard verbs of action. I cause it to be the case that there is a camel in my living-room, which I then cause to rise into the air because of the effect of little hydrogen balloons tied to its extremities. We might describe this also by saying that I brought a camel into my living-room and raised it into the air by attaching the balloons to it. Typically, the action verbs give more information that the 'brought about' idioms, by committing themselves to assertions about the means by which the effect is produced. They are biased towards the standard modes of human agency. (This has been remarked on by several recent writers with respect to the difference between 'kill' and 'cause to die'.)

In explaining actions, then, we can find ourselves explaining events of any kind. The assertion 'he did it' serves as an intermediate step in the explanation, connecting the explanation of why he did it with the event that he produced, and indicating that the explanation of this event is to be found in states of the agent. The first important result of this is that the vocabulary in which actions are described ranges through our whole vocabulary for describing the world, and the constructions involved can range through our grammar. If I say that a brought about the simultaneous destruction of all the bridges except the one which looks as if the designer was trying to express a reaction to the smallness of his commission, then I am crediting a with bringing about an event to describe which I need quantification over time, a number of sentential connectives, and an embedded-sentence construction. Any explanation of a's action will have to be itself involved enough to have consequences of this complexity.

Suppose now that we have a variety of actions, involving

events expressed by sentences a_1, a_2, . . ., performed by an agent a, and a theory θ, either about the agent or about human nature, which is to explain them. Presumably the explanations make use of a variety of sets of incidental facts, C_1, C_2, . . ., such that C_i conjoined with θ explains a_i. I take the relation to be deductive, so that, for each i, C_i conjoined with θ entails a_i.

θ will be expressed in a particular vocabulary; there will be only so many predicates in it. The a_i may together contain an indefinitely large vocabulary; every predicate in the language may occur in some a_i. How then can θ explain the a_i? Deductive relations from θ to the whole range of the a_i will have to go from the limited vocabulary of θ to the potentially unlimited vocabulary of the set a_1, a_2, ...

Suppose first that θ is a first-order theory. It contains no intensional terms or higher order terms such as quantifiers over predicates. Suppose further not only that the a_i contain terms not found in θ but that some of them contain only such terms. Suppose that a typical a_i is expressed in predicates not found in θ. This is certainly the case when the a_i are actions and θ is a formal or informal psychological theory; most descriptions of actions refer only to features of the environment that have no psychological content. We then have to worry about the theorem that if a consistent set of first-order sentences S entails a non-tautologous sentence t then S and t have vocabulary in common. Whatever entails *all* of the a_i must itself range all over the vocabulary of the language, and not just over that of θ.

One way in which this can be accomplished, still taking θ to be a first-order theory, is for the deductive burden imposed by the range of vocabulary of the a_i to be borne by the incidental conditions C_1, C_2, . . . Thus θ may be 'when John is sleepy he yawns'

C_1: John was sleepy on Tuesday

C_2: John was sleepy on Wednesday at the concert and a yawn at a concert leads to a disturbance

C_3: John was sleepy on Thursday while listening to the chairman, who is offended by yawns

And the actions explained:

a_1: John yawned on Tuesday

a_2: John disturbed the concert on Wednesday

a_3: John offended the chairman on Thursday.

Another way is to take the theory θ *not* to be a single theory, a finitely long set of assumptions with a limited vocabulary, but a collection of theories, each sub-theory being 'improvised' to fit the needs of explaining some a_i.

Both of these methods are in fact used in everyday psychology; we do use a great variety of incidental environmental conditions, and we do improvise explanations to suit particular circumstances. Used alone, though, neither will capture the concept of agency, in that neither will assert that the common factor in the actions a_i is the activity of the agent who produces them. Or, to put the point differently, these principles will not allow us to take account of the fact that even had external conditions been exactly as they were, the action would have been performed differently had something about the agent been different. We ask not just why someone did something but why it was done *as* it was done; we ask how it was done. And the main burden of all these adverbial modifications of action descriptions is to describe variations and details which can only be due to facts about the agent rather than the environment.[2]

'Why did you offend the chairman last Thursday?'

'Well, I was sleepy and I yawned; you know I always do when I get the least bit tired. And that really offends old stiff-face.'

'But why did you do it so definitively? You could have caught yourself in the middle of it, or apologized, or later been especially agreeable.'

'Oh, I suppose I enjoy annoying him, and I didn't think there was any way of saving the situation, anyway.'

The remaining strategy is not to construe θ as a first-order theory at all. And this is what I think we do when we explain action in a way that brings out the characteristic facts of agency. It is clear how a higher-order theory expressed in a

---

[2] There is a connection here, though indirect, with Anthony Kenny's discussion of adverbial modification in *Action, Emotion, and Will* (Routledge, London, 1969), and Donald Davidson's development of Kenny's point, in 'The Logical Form of Action Sentences' in *The Logic of Action and Decision*, N. Rescher, ed., (Pittsburgh U.P., Pittsburgh, 1967).

limited vocabulary can have consequences which involve an unlimited range of predicates. For the theory may contain principles that quantify over properties or propositions, and then an unlimited range of predicates will result just by universal instantiation. Now it is essential to note that common-sense psychological idioms almost never involve literally higher-order constructions. The higher-order devices are usually disguised, and there are a number of ways of doing this.

One of the simplest such idioms expresses attitudes to activities or actions (the category *Att* of Chapter II). Explanatory principles involving this category usually take the form of a quantification over actions or activities.

For example, θ: If he enjoys doing something, he does it.

c_1: He enjoys gambling.

a_1: He's gambling.

(θ is not a tautology; it would be false of many agents.)

I find it interesting that concepts such as that of enjoyment have both motivational and cognitive content; they seem to have elements of both desire and belief. 'Because he likes to' is a perfectly self-sufficient explanation; 'because he believes p' or 'because he wants q' require completion, though the completion can often remain tacit, with a statement of desire (for the belief) or belief (for the desire). When we want a more indirect connection between the explained action and the states of the agent, when we want more room to stick in explanatory details, we have to split primitive attitudes to activities into belief and desire.

It is in the second-order quality of psychological concepts that I see the origin of their intensionality. I shall explain how this is to work in the special case of belief. At this point, though, I can make a grand conjecture about the classification of psychological terms in common sense. I can't establish it, but it is grand enough and plausible enough to unveil.

I think that nearly all everyday psychological terms have a disguised higher-order form. And that the natural classification of them is in terms of the form of the disguise. With attitudes to action the disguise takes the form of predications of actions;

but actions are things whose descriptions embed sentences. With belief and desire the disguise takes the form of a commentary on an embedded sentence; but when we take a look at explanatory principles involving beliefs and desires we find that the quantification over propositions has got turned into one over their contents. This quantification over individuals is thus (or so I shall argue) a disguised quantification over both properties and individuals.

I am not able to go through the categories of Chapter II, redescribing each as a mode of disguise of an essentially higher-order idiom. Even if it cannot be done (and I suspect very strongly that it can be done) the core of the idea remains. It is that common sense was faced with an explanatory situation in which higher-order principles were needed. And so instead of inventing second-order quantifiers it invented embedded sentences. And then it was faced with the need for finer syntactical distinctions, in order to make enough distinctions, to have enough space, to explain the details of actions, and so we end up with a multitude of modes of sentence embedding, in part corresponding to the maze of devices of nominalization that grammarians try to sort out.

PREINTENSIONALITY

The aim is to show how belief is a higher-order concept. The first element in the formula is common to belief and to considerably less involved concepts, such as love, jealousy, hate, fear. These concepts appear to assert a relation between an agent and an object of his interest. '*a* is jealous of *b*.' The 'relation' however is not such an innocent business. Suppose that it is true of *a* that if he is jealous of some person then he will be scrupulously polite to that person. The principle is apparently of the form $(x)(J(a, x) \supset P(a, x))$, a simple universal quantification. If *a* is jealous of *b* then *a* will be polite to *b*; but not if *b* appears in disguise and misbehaves, or if *b* has another identity under which he plays another role in *a*'s life. (*a* is jealous of the professor he corresponds with, not knowing him to be the same as the drinking friend he likes to abuse.)

For any *b* one can tell the story so that *a* is jealous of someone who happens to be *b* and yet is polite to *b*. Is the general principle false of *a* then? No. No more than similar general principles of belief, e.g. 'if *a* thinks that someone has accomplished something he failed at, *a* will be carefully admiring of the fact' are. The fact is that both belief and a number of other idioms, some of which do not in their surface grammar involve embedded sentences, share a feature that I shall call *preintensionality*, of being subject to a curiously intensional form of quantification. A definition of preintensionality is in effect given by the formal treatment at the end of this section; it will be enough to say now that a preintensional idiom behaves as if quantification brings out a hidden propositional content. Besides the simple relational quality there seems to be some other element, which blocks the inference 'R(a) and (x)(R(x) $\supset$ S(x)) therefore S(a)'.

If concepts such as love, jealousy, and hatred were not preintensional we could not formulate principles relating them to belief and desire, such as 'if *a* loves someone, he will suspect that she despises him'. It is worth noting explicitly that preintensionality does not entail intensionality. *a* is jealous of his drinking friend, though he does not know that his drinking friend is the person he is jealous of. The absence of an explicit propositional content makes it impossible to formulate the classical focus of intensionality: if we add such a content—and say that *a* is jealous that the professor he writes to can get away with such absurdities, but is not jealous that his drinking friend can get away with such absurdities—then intensionality is immediate. Descriptions are part of propositions.

Preintensionality corresponds to the most basic element of belief, acquaintance. We say that *a* is acquainted with *b*, or that *a* knows about *b* (or, more strongly, I feel, that *a* knows who *b* is). Acquaintance is required in order to have a belief about something, and it seems clear that one cannot love or be jealous of something one is not acquainted with. But acquaintance is obviously not a simple relation between a person and an object. It is itself a preintensional relation; the mother of them all, in fact.

It is important to see that any concept can appear intensional, given the right stage setting. It makes perfect sense to say 'Hamlet stabbed, not the sententious fool who had so often roused his boredom and annoyance, but the mysterious figure moving threateningly behind the arras'. We set things up this way when we are preparing to apply belief or some similar concept, and often the intensionality really belongs with the belief. That is, a trivial paraphrase makes the idiom of belief (desire, attempt . . .) the only intensional element, and this paraphrase clearly gives better truth conditions for the sentence in question. 'Hamlet was not trying to kill Polonius, he did not know that he was behind the arras; he thought that there was a spy there and tried, successfully, to stab him.' In claiming that non-propositional attitudes like love or jealousy are preintensional I am claiming more than this trivial expressibility in (misleadingly) intensional terms. The claim is that the semantic apparatus appropriate for belief is needed to clarify their logic too. More specifically, that the same concept of acquaintance is required.

One can be acquainted with something, one can know of it, in many different ways. I have no intention of cataloguing them. The ways in which acquaintance is obtained do have to compose into a unity, however. That is, we may take each person to be at the centre of a network of referential relations, which tie him to the things he can think about or have attitudes towards. The relations themselves are indefinitely disparate (one sees things, one hears things spoken of, one deduces their existence, . . .); but they must be knitted together into a coherent structure. No single relation can be one of acquaintance unless it is capable of being composed with other acquaintanceships into this net. What this amounts to, I think, is two main conditions on referential relations. There are algebraic conditions that ensure that the relations compose to form a network. No doubt these are really very subtle. I extract from all that one might say about them just this: There is associated with a person a set of binary relations $R_1, R_2, \ldots$, and a set of objects related by the relations; the objects may include besides the person himself and objects in his environment abstract objects and psychological entities, such as mentally asserted tokens of names or sentences. Then we extend the set of R_i by adding to it any relation which can be defined as a set of ordered pairs the first of which is always connected by a chain of R_i to the second. (In other words, one object is referentially related to another when you can get from the first to the second by a chain of relations from the R_i, and a referential relation is any subrelation of referential relatedness as just defined.) Then there are causal conditions that ensure that this network form the acquaintanceship of a person. I shall extract from these just that the network centre on the person, and that it associate with its termini features of the objects of acquaintance. The first of these can be expressed by requiring that if a is the person then any object that bears a referential relation to any other, or which some other object bears a referential relation to, be related by some referential relation to a. And the second of these can be expressed by requiring that whenever a referential relation R ties a to an object o then there be a set of properties of o, call it $R(o)$, associated with R and o.

I shall use capital R, S, . . . as variables over referential relations. In asserting that a is acquainted with o, one asserts that a bears some R to o. In asserting that a bears some pre-intensional relation to o (for example jealousy or love) one is asserting that there is some R such that a bears this relation to o as presented to it by R. In effect one has a three-place relation between a, o, and R. The o and the R are not treated as being this independent of each other by ordinary language, though, and so I shall write the basic relation $L(a, o/R)$. ('a loves o as presented by R.') The point is that in the use of preintensional concepts one almost never treats the o and the R places completely independently. One quantifies them both together, and further specification of the R place is presented as a qualification of a. Thus one has:

a is jealous of o: $\exists R(J(a, o/R) \ \& \ R(a, o))$

a is jealous of everyone: $(x) \ (R) \ (R(a, x) \supset J(a, x/R))$

a is jealous of Sam, as winner of the contest:

$\exists R(\hat{x} \text{ wins the contest} \in R(s) \ \& \ R(a, s) \ \& \ J(a, s/R))$

('some R is associated with winning, leads to s, and via it
  a is jealous of s')

What we have here is evidently an instance of the common-
sense strategy I discussed earlier, of attaching reference to
properties to reference to individuals, so that a more manageable
syntax serves to present a semantically very complex second-
order content. One result is a limitation of the expressive power
of the idīom, though; there's no easy way in English to say
$(x)\exists R\ J(a,\ x/R)$, and the like: the objects and the referential
relations have to stay very much in step. Another consequence
is preintensionality; a can be jealous of o *qua* winner of the
contest and not jealous of o *qua* the man he meets at the bus stop.
This may not seem a very substantial sort of intensionality; it
isn't satisfyingly mysterious in its content or exotic in the object
it appeals to. But it is of a piece with the intensionality of belief,
according to the next section.

SENTENTIALITY

To have a belief about something is more than to be related in
some way to it as presented by some referential relation. For in
belief acquaintance is bundled up in claims about the way the
world is; one has all the elements of a sentence, and most
importantly their composition together, to deal with, and not
just single referring terms. Yet if we take all but a single term
as constant in a belief we are left with something much like a
preintensional relation. Consider 'a believes of b that-he-has-
hurt-him' or 'a suspects c of-being-his-anonymous-benefactor'.
Another way of describing the transition from preintensionality
to sentence containment is therefore this: a sentence-embedding
such as that of belief allows one to construct arbitrarily many
preintensional contexts, by embedding different sentences and
then considering different terms in these sentences as occupying
generalizable argument places. (So that just as we have the
explanatory principle 'if Sam is jealous of someone he will be
unusually polite to them', we have 'if Sam suspects someone of-
being-cruel-to-cats, then he will lose all respect for them'.) How
is this capacity obtained?

A helpful formulation is due to Bertrand Russell. Russell[3] paraphrases '*a* believes that Othello loves Desdemona' as 'Othello is related by *a*'s representation of the relation of loving to Desdemona'. There are no end of problems with this formulation. It ignores most forms of intensionality, since it allows free substitution for 'Othello' and 'Desdemona'; it can apply only on the supposition that all of the names refer (making Russell's choice of example unfortunate); and it is only applicable to very simple syntactical forms. Yet there is something right about it. What seems attractive about Russell's formulation is the attempt to make the relatedness to objects that results from belief to be a central part of the analysis rather than something that one struggles to make a consequence of an attitude to a proposition. What seems misguided is the taking of the referential or representational relation as unstructured, transparent.

Begin with a belief whose content is a simple relation between two actual individuals. Robert believes that Johannes loves Clara. Robert is acquainted with Johannes and with Clara, relative to two relations of acquaintance, and for that matter Robert is acquainted with love. So for some R, S, T, R(r, j), S(r, c), and T(r, L). And Robert's belief about these objects of his acquaintance has a particular form, expressed by the application of the relation of love to these two people. That device of the language, application of predicates to arguments, is probably not something Robert is acquainted with. We can associate with it a relation between acquaintance relations. So, suppressing the argument-place for Robert, and calling the new relation C: C(T, R, S). That is to say 'Robert applies the object of T to the objects of R and S'.

Most generally, we could take the form of believed predication to be C(r, R, σ), holding when r is a person who applies the predicate that is the object of R to the objects of the first n places of the sequence σ of referential relations (where n is the number of places of the object of R).

[3] 'The Nature of Truth and Falsehood', in *Philosophical Essays* (Allen and Unwin, London, 1966).

What, now, when Robert believes that Johannes does not love Clara, or believes that Johannes loves Clara and Clara does not love Johannes? Let us begin with the case of negation. It is perfectly possible for there to be a relation of believed non-predication, holding between people, relations-as-represented, and objects-as-represented. $C(R, S, T)$ would hold when the person in question doubts (disbelieves) that the object of R relates those of S and T. With sufficient ingenuity, one can extend this account to more complex cases. The whole thing becomes very unnatural and hard to have faith in, though. Implausible as the approach is in general, it seems a real possibility in some cases where we want to minimize demands on the referential relations. We say of a small child who understands just a little language that he disbelieves that Daddy is home, when someone says 'Daddy's home' and he mistrusts the report. We are probably not ascribing any of the simpler and more sophisticated relations that follow immediately below, but rather just saying that the child relates his representations of Daddy and of presence in a manner of disbelief.

Negation is generally better represented as follows. Robert believes of not-loving that it holds between Clara and Johannes. To put this formally, we have to refer both to referential relations and to their objects:

$\exists R\ \exists S\ \exists T\ (R(r, \{<x, y>: x$ does not love $y\})\ \&\ S(r, c)\ \&$
    $T(r, j)\ \&\ C(R, S, T)$.

And similarly 'Robert believes that Johannes loves Clara and Clara does not love Johannes', where all that follows the 'that' is the content of one belief, *may* be taken as:

$\exists R\ \exists S\ \exists T\ (R(r, \{<x, y, z, w>: x$ loves y and y does not love
    $x)\ \&\ S(r, j)\ \&\ T(r, c)\ \&\ C(R, S, T))$.

The same sentence may be taken in other ways. For example as

$\exists R\ \exists S\ (R(r, \{x: x$ loves $c\ \&\ c$ does not love $x\})\ \&\ S(r, j)\ \&$
    $C(R, S))$

or even as

$\exists R\ \exists S\ (R(r, \{x: x = x\ \&\ j$ loves $c\ \&\ c$ does not love $y\})\ \&$
    $S(r, r)\ \&\ C(R, S))$.

It is clear that as we approach the last of these the referential relation R is coming to play the role of a propositional object of belief. And, closely related to this, it is clear that the whole approach consists in shifting the burden of analysis from the relation of believed predication to the referential relations.

REFERENTIAL RELATIONS AS PROPOSITIONS

How does one represent the relation of not loving? Supposing that one represents the relation of loving, the simplest way of extending the reference to not-loving is to know the place of verbal tokens of 'doesn't love' in the structure of inferences. 'know' here must be largely a matter of knowing how rather than knowing that, if it is to support the representation that supports belief. One has to recognize the antipathy between assertions of 'loves' and 'doesn't love'. This is certainly not the only way of acquiring a representation of not loving. One can learn the extension of it as a primitive term, especially if it is a commoner feature of one's environment than love is. One can learn to disbelieve 'doesn't love' of those of whom one believes 'loves' if one possesses a primitive relation of disbelieving. It seems to me, though, that understanding the inferential role of negation is the only way in which one can possess a general way of representing the negation of any relation one can represent. The ascription of more than the occasional negative belief to a creature without fairly complex linguistic capacities will thus not be plausible.

The variety of ways in which one can come to be acquainted with an extension seems as varied, as interestingly varied, as the ways in which reference to individuals is achieved. In fact, reference to individuals represents the special case in which the extension consists of just one thing. At the opposite limit there are expressions that syntactically seem to designate extensions, but which have a proposition-like sense, such as 'being self-identical and Johannes loves Clara', as readers of Frege or Davidson will appreciate. Such expressions certainly do not *designate* propositions, if we take them extensionally, for if Johannes loves Clara the set of objects that are self-identical and Johannes loves Clara is exactly the same as the set of objects that are self-identical and $2+2=4$. And so for any two truths.

What one is related to in believing, though, is not just the objects of one's acquaintance, but the objects as presented to one by various relations. To be acquainted with an object via R is not to be acquainted with it via S, even though the two relations connect the same objects. Robert in believing that Johannes loves Clara may mentally connect presentations of Johannes and Clara with a representation of love, and he may also apply a representation of loving Clara to one of Johannes, and he may even apply a representation of being such that Johannes loves Clara to himself or to the world. If he is rational and patient and has the resources for forming all these representations he will do all of these. To form the more complex representations Robert needs a linguistic medium and a grasp of its conventions. He can represent the relation of loving by taking part in social relations and in understanding literature. He can represent Clara and Johannes by frequent contact with them. He can represent loving Clara by reflection on the instances of it around him. And he can represent being such that Johannes loves Clara by tying the parts of the sentence 'Johannes loves Clara' to these other representations, to get an attribute, of anything indifferently, that he can take as a proposition.

But he does not *have* to do any but the simplest of these feats to believe that Johannes loves Clara and is not loved in return. That is, his belief can amount to the first of the construals I gave of it rather than any of the later ones. The complex proposition-like object of acquaintance is therefore nearly always redundant; the property-as-represented that it represents will almost never be an object of acquaintance unless the believer is also acquainted with the simpler properties that one would refer to in stating the proposition. And then it is the structure of the believer's acquaintance with these that forms the substance of his belief.

INTENSIONALITY

My strategy for dealing with the intensionality of belief is pretty evident now. Robert believes that Johannes loves Clara, but he does not believe that the composer of his favourite tune loves Clara. For Robert is related in one way, direct day-to-day acquaintance, with Johannes, and via this relation he does connect Johannes with loving Clara. And he is related in another less immediate way to Johannes, via his memory of a tune whose authorship he has forgotten, and he does not connect Johannes via this relation with loving Clara. $C(T, R, U)$ is true, where R is the first of these relations and T and U connect r with loving and Clara, while $C(T, S, U)$ is false, where S is the second relation, though both relations relate r to the same object.

This is straightforward enough when the statement that ascribes the belief indicates the relations involved. 'I thought that my new employer was likely to be keeping tabs on me, but it never crossed my mind that this little character beside me in the battered hat was he, and carefully noting everything I did.' It is more confusing when we have no such indication, as in the classical examples from Frege to Quine. Hugo believes that Cicero denounced Cataline, but not that Tully denounced Cataline. We cannot immediately find what the two different referential relations must be, via which Hugo does and does not represent Cicero–Tully as denouncing Cataline. But really there is nothing essentially different here. Hugo is related to Cicero–Tully by one relation, via which he does believe of him that he denounced Cataline, and also related to him by another, via which he does not. We need not know what these two relations are. $\exists R \, (R(h, c) \, \& \, C(h, T, R))$ and $\exists R \, (R(h, c) \, \& \sim C \, (h, T, R))$ may both be true.

If Hugo believes that Cicero, and not Tully, denounced Cataline, it may not be that he takes 'Cicero' to mean 'the man who P' and 'Tully' to mean 'the man who Q'. He may, for example, have met 'Cicero' in a book on the Cataline conspiracy, and never actually have heard of 'Tully' before being asked if Tully denounced Cataline, but vaguely associate it with some half-remembered lines of Catullus ('Dissertissime Romuli nepotum/Quot sunt quotque fuere, Marce Tulli').

A subject-predicate sentence of the form 'r believes that a is B' thus asserts that r takes a to fall under B, where both a and B are related to r by referential relations which may or may not be indicated in the sentence itself. If a is named by a description as in 'r believes that the man running up to him is his cousin', then we can often, but not always, take the content of the description to indicate the relation in question. But where the referent is indicated just by a name or by a description that is clearly more part of what is said of the object than a specification of what it is said of ('r believes that Seneca was an old fake'), then no such indication is given us. Given thus only the resources of the notation 'r believes that a is B' there can never be an answer to the question of when 'r believes that a is B' and '$a = b$' entail 'r believes that b is A'. The notation leaves out the information that is essential to answering the question, namely the referential relations that r bears to a and their association with the names a and b. And given this information the answer is trivial, the inference goes through when both belief sentences involve the same referential relation. Ordinary language does not usually leave out this information, but it has no uniform way of presenting it.

The content of any ascription of belief must in part depend on information that is not given automatically by the use of 'believes'. There must be a set of very delicate conventions that relate the use of information surrounding the assertion of a belief sentence to the subtleties of the grammatical form of the sentence. But what the form of these conventions is, I am not foolish enough to conjecture.

QUANTIFICATIONS

We now have the tools for half-solving a number of problems about belief. I mean that in many puzzling cases, notably the logical form of quantified belief sentences and the content of beliefs about fictional or mythical objects, we are in a position to state a plausible position which requires just one little obscurity, one quick gesture in the direction of more ultimately to be said, to make it work.

A wide-scope quantified belief sentence, 'There is someone whom Robert believes to love Clara', should, according to what I have said, be taken as 'there is someone related to Robert by some referential relation, via which Robert predicates love of Clara to him'. (I ignore Robert's referential connection to Clara and to Love.) And the evident objection to this is that it will be true as long as there is any referring term *a* such that 'Robert believes that *a* loves Clara' is true. There is a considerable literature, to some of which I referred in footnote 1, above, attesting to the fact that we usually require more for the truth of the existential quantification in such contexts than just that an instance be true. If Robert believes that whoever left his hat on the piano loves Clara then he believes that someone loves Clara without believing of someone that he loves Clara. On the other hand, I have argued elsewhere (see footnote 1) that we must come very near to sometimes allowing the simple truth of an instance to establish quantifiability if we are to hold as true various very ordinary explanatory principles. An interesting example of such a principle, full of instructive traps, is 'if Robert believes that someone loves Clara he will try to discover who that person is'. (The scope really is wide; it reads 'if a person is such that Robert believes of them that they love Clara then Robert will try to discover their identity'.)

The way out of the situation is pretty clear, though, in outline. When we insist that there is someone of whom Robert believes ϕ, rather than contenting ourselves with the less cumbersome 'Robert believes that someone is ϕ', the trouble we are going to indicates something special about the connection between Robert and the someone. Robert is related to that person by a referential relation with some special feature. *What* special feature may not be immediately discoverable; we may have to wait and learn more. If the assertion is a preparation for an appeal to some explanatory principle, such as 'Robert will be very guarded with anyone he thinks loves Clara', then the purpose of the original clumsy idiom was to make it possible later to impose as a special condition on the referential relation that it should be capable of making this principle true. For Robert's belief that x loves Clara will only lead him to be guarded with that person if the relation R via which he believes this allows him to recognize that person in a situation in which one might be guarded. In the notation of an earlier section, R(x) must include information on the basis of which Robert may recognize x face to face.

A different explanatory principle may require a different construal of the conditions on a referential relation.'If Robert believes that someone loves Clara he will try to find out who he is' is a case in point. Here the relation certainly does not have to provide recognizability; unrecognizability is just the situation it presupposes. Perhaps in some circumstances this principle can be made true by any referential relation between Robert and his acquaintances. I think, though, that it does impose a rather weak restriction on such relations. The abstract belief that someone loves Clara, perhaps based on the general conviction that everyone is loved by someone, does not seem quite enough, and so Robert's belief that 'whoever loves Clara' (or, following Kaplan 'the youngest person to love Clara') loves Clara does not seem to count. A qualifying x must be conceivably track-downable; R(x) must present information that would allow Robert to begin a search for x. In any case, these requirements are clearly much weaker than those for the first principle I cited, and so we can have quantified assertions in which they clash, for example 'There's someone Robert believes to love Clara, and he is trying to discover who he is, but since he doesn't yet know who he is he may for all he knows be treating him unguardedly every day.' It would be hard to construe this as consistent, and impossible to construe it as consistent with both explanatory principles alluded to, without taking into account the fact that there are different referential relations qualified by different conditions. (Cf. the discussion of the orange lipstick murderer in Chapter IV.)

To sum up, a sentence such as 'there is someone of whom Robert believes ϕ' typically has the form

∃x∃R(R(r, x) & r predicates ϕ of x via R & Σ(R))

or, adapting the notation of the preintensionality section,

∃x∃R(Believes$_r$ ϕ(x/R) & Σ(R))

where Σ can be any of a range of conditions specified contextually. One important contextual element is the presence of explanatory principles. Some of them have the appearance 'if Robert believes ϕ of some x, then ψ(x)'. This may represent any of the following:

(a) (x)(R)(Believes$_r$ ϕ(x/R) ⊃ ψ(x))

(b) (x)(R)((Believes$_r$ ϕ(x/R) & Γ(R)) ⊃ ψ(x))

(c) ∃R(x)(Believes$_r$ ϕ(x/R) ⊃ ψ(x))

or even

(d) ∃R(x)(Γ(R) & (Believes$_r$ ϕ(x/R) ⊃ ψ(x)))

You won't discover which of these is the right one in a particular case, or what Γ amounts to, by reflecting on logical form. 'If Robert thinks that someone loves Clara he will try to discover who he is' has the form

(e) (x)(R)((Believes$_r$ loves(x/R, c) & Γ(R)) ⊃ Try$_r$ ∃S(Believes$_r$ loves (x/S, c) & Σ(S))

where Γ is a weak condition and Σ is a strong one. The coincidence of the doubling of conditions on referential relations with the double embedding of intensional contexts in the consequent seems to me very significant, but I shall not pursue it.

NON-EXISTENTS

In describing the difference between 'Robert believes that someone loves Clara' and 'there is someone whom Robert believes to love Clara' I did not say that the former and not the latter presupposes that there actually is such a person. For while I think that in many cases successful reference is required for the truth of a wide-scope quantification of this kind, I am not sure that there is any such general presupposition. For we seem to gloss over the difference between existence and non-existence in ordinary psychological explanation when for example we explain some of Robert's actions by saying that maddened by jealousy he hypothesized a definite particular, but quite non-existent, lover for Clara and then, in accordance with principles already mentioned, proceeded to search for him. I think moreover that I know how it is that we manage to lose sight of real existence here and still use explanatory principles that appear to require it. If in the formalization (e) above we just drop the 'x' in 'x/R' and 'x/S' we get a syntactically coherent principle:

(R)(Believes$_r$ loves (R, c) & Γ(R)) $\supset$ Try$_r$ $\exists$S(Believes$_r$ loves (S, c) & Σ(S))

(Note that this would not be true of the simpler principles (a), (b), (c), (d). One needs a sentence-embedding context in the consequent so that the overlap of propositional content can provide the required cross reference. Note also that if (e), or (a)–(d) modified to obtain such propositional cross-reference, were fully formalized along the lines I suggested in the 'Sententiality' section, cross-reference would be accomplished by variables over referential relations to the components of these propositional contents.)

The sense of the reformulated principle is that the agent's action is explained by his relation to various referential relations, without taking into account what objects these referential relations terminate in. This is plausible enough in many cases. Successful reference usually involves a whole network of conjoined referential relations. The network involves many non-terminal nodes which have representational content: beliefs, books, stories, images. One can thus truncate the system of referential relations. leaving as terminal nodes of the network nodes that are not in fact terminal. (See the diagram on p. 119.) These then can serve the role of real objects of reference in any explanatory context in which it is the agent's ability to manage the apparatus of reference, to find routes round the web of belief, rather than to interact with particular real objects, that is crucial.

The self-sufficiency of the referential network, the way it can come to usurp the place of the objects it connects one with as a human concern and in the formation of sentential attitudes, is a familiar business. Intuitions about it lie behind the perennial seductiveness of idealism, and vocabulary that expresses it also usually summons, I feel, intuitions from various essentially social tensions between the use of the (social, conceptual)

ROBERT, CLARA, JOHANNES, AND THE REFERENTIAL NETWORK

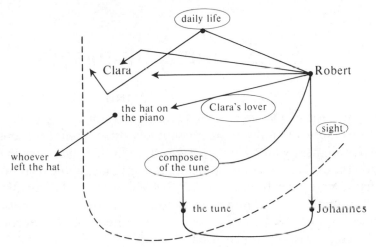

Relations via which Robert's beliefs can refer to objects are marked →. There are beliefs and descriptions associated with them which may be alluded to in a sentence ascribing belief. Robert believes of Johannes via the relation marked 'composer of the tune' that he loves Clara, but not via the relation marked 'sight'. If the system of relations and their nodes is truncated along the dotted line, Robert's more suspicious beliefs retain their intelligibility although now we are not construing him as moved by beliefs about the real objects of reference. Clara, inevitably, is the terminus of so many relations and is an intermediate point of his reference to so many other things, that she is to him, as he is to himself, hardly distinguishable from the network itself. The more an agent's beliefs are tied together by relations of inference, the greater the number of such truncations there will be, which leave sufficient structure to explain the agent's actions.

apparatus of reference and the (physical, practical) manipulation of things. I would like to be able to express this better, to make it respectable and abstruse. And while there is certainly more to say along the lines of the remarks on psychological explanation of these last two sections, a really informative treatment will have to await a more thorough treatment of themes from earlier in this appendix. The first prerequisite would be an explicit formulation of the algebraic conditions on referential relations. The second would be a theory of the skills required to use the network that results from their algebraic composition.

V

THE PLASTICITY OF DESIRE

WANTING AND ACTING

An analysis of the concept of action might not be expected to tell us more about desire than about any other mental concept. After all, nearly all mental concepts have as their main occupation the explanation of what we do. In fact, though, the relations that actions bear to one another, between simple and complex actions and between means and ends, reveal a structure that is essentially connected to the structuring of items in the category of desire: wishes, wants, needs, intentions. And it is only by reference to this structure that we can understand the ways in which actions are explained as results of the percolation of desire and belief.

The general idea may be gathered from an example. Someone is writing a letter while talking to a friend and cleaning his pipe. Each of these three actions is a scattered collection, and the little temporally continuous parts of each of them may be continuous with parts of others; the gestures of the conversation and the motion of the pipe-cleaner may be linked. But we ignore these continuities, or at any rate treat them as details, fine structure, and piece things together differently, perhaps against the natural, balletic, turnings of the physical movements, to get parts of writing, talking, cleaning, and to put these together into the larger whole acts. The reason we do this is perfectly clear; we articulate actions in order to set them up for explanation, and we have definite ideas about the form that a psychological explanation should take and the kinds of motives and intentions that are likely to be found behind the goings-on in question. The reasons for writing, talking, cleaning are likely to be units, and they are likely to be refined into the reasons for the natural subdivisions of these actions.

It may be plausible, then, that the ways in which we group and dissect actions reflect presuppositions about how they are to be explained, and that in particular cases the articulation of actions will reveal an articulation of the desires motivating them. It is not clear, yet, that there are any organizing notions built into the concepts of action and desire to orchestrate their accord, or even that it is the concept ot desire that is particularly implicated.

THE ARTICULATION OF ACTION

We do not take actions to follow one another as a sequence of independent events, each occasioned just by what precedes it. The successive productions of notes in a performance of a piece of music are not taken as an unstructured series. We phrase them into runs and arpeggios; we not only group them into units, we articulate these units into phrases and sub-phrases and sub-sub-phrases. We *give* actions a sort of a syntax; the phrasing is easily redescribed as a tree. It seems clear, too, that we read actions in this way for good reason; actions are in fact governed by processes that organize them into hierarchies of groupings. The psychological facts seem to be that whole sequences of actions are prepared as wholes, and their parts co-ordinated in advance. The evidence for this is just about conclusive in the case of speech. (The simplest forms of evidence are the determinate forms that slips of the tongue take, and the basic physiology of the vocal apparatus. Transmission of a signal to the larynx for the production of one phoneme must occur in the brain simultaneously with the transmission of a signal to the tongue for a *preceding* phoneme.) And the evidence is extremely telling for other complex, co-ordinated actions such as typing or playing an instrument.[1]

Lashley used considerations of this sort in 1951 to argue that behaviourist analyses of action were implausible. Lashley's

---

[1] See K. S. Lashley, 'The Problem of Serial Order in Behavior', in L. A. Jeffress, ed., *Cerebral Mechanisms in Behavior* (Wiley, New York, 1951), J. Fodor, M. F. Garrett, T. G. Bever, *The Psychology of Language* (McGraw-Hill, New York, 1974), Chapter 7, and Henry Shaffer, 'Intention and Performance', *Psychological Review* 83, 1976.

considerations show very clearly why it is that the concept of a behavioural response is intuitively not much of a substitute for that of an action. Built into the concept of an action is the idea of hierarchical organization. I shall take this to be a very basic part of the common-sense idea of action (so that what Lashley was arguing was that on this point common sense has the psychological facts on its side). A more particular part of the idea, that this organization corresponds to the relation between the various motives underlying the action, may seem appropriate enough for planned intentional physical movements, but is not nearly so evident for, say, unintentional actions or actions that are causally very distant from bodily motions. My aim in this section is to lay out the idea, to describe the organization I take to be basic to action and its relations to the agent's motives, in such a way that its ubiquity is plausible.

Consider a musical rational agent playing the oboe in public. He plays mostly from the music before him, improvising the ornamentation as he goes along. (It's a Handel sonata.) He plans the performance of each phrase before he gets to it: this loud and cheerful, this dark and wispy. As he plays through each phrase he adjusts his embouchure, tonguing, and breath control to get the effect he had wanted and to make the thing turn out well as it goes along. His audience hears the music as music, articulated more or less as the performer intended, and takes the performance as a performance, with its own articulations corresponding in part to those of the music. Some of the audience may be aware of the oboist's tonguing and fingering; these constitute more actions to be taken as co-articulated with the rest of the performance.

All these are perfect examples of action, just the kind of thing that the concept of action most easily applies to, I think. They are perfect in a number of ways. First of all, they are *animated* in the way that anything we take as an action must ultimately be. One cannot hear the music, any more than one can watch a dance or an animal stalking, without taking there to be active co-ordinating processes behind, somehow *in*, them. Then, they are *performances* in a straightforward way. Each consists in the fact that an event has occurred as a result of the agent's bringing it about; a statement of each has the form, not 'e happened', but '*a* did e'. What does this doing, bringing about, consist in? Not just in any causal relation between the event and the agent's intentions, as a little reflection shows the causal relation has to be of a particular kind. I would claim it to consist in the event's resulting from the agent's co-articulation of all he is doing and wanting, but this will have to be spelt out and argued for. And, lastly, they are connected to one another as actions typically are. The agent relaxes his embouchure during a crescendo *in order* not to go sharp; he gets that mysterious dark sound *by* a combination of a particular vibrato and some mysteriously controllable relation between his tongue and his sinuses; *in* playing a phrase staccato he contrasts it with the previous one.[2]

The musician in the example will have performed many other actions as well as those I have mentioned. Many of them will be much less direct reflections of the genesis of the agent's intentions, either because of the limits of his knowledge or because of the resistance of the environment to his efforts, what Sartre called its 'coefficient of adversity'. For example, in playing the sonata as he does he offends an influential critic, who writes a hostile review; in playing the last movement his reed becomes unresponsive and so, after trying unsuccessfully to do a clean sforzando, he gives up and plays the rest of the movement much less dramatically than the score seems to indicate. ('Very interesting,' say his friends; 'a travesty,' says the critic.) These, offending the critic, messing up the sforzando, playing the last movement undramatically, are clearly actions, too. But they are less plausibly described as articulations, of the agent's motions or of his use of some medium. That is, I think, one does not as readily see behind them a hierarchical structure of

---

[2] Other analyses of action which emphasize some of the same points are found in Donald Davidson, 'The Logical Form of Action Sentences', in *The Logic of Action and Decision*, N. Rescher, ed. (Pittsburgh U.P., 1967), and in Chapter 2 of Alvin Goldman's *A Theory of Human Action* (Princeton U.P., 1970). Neither writer would want to be implicated in my identification of actions with the results of the co-ordination of behaviour.

intentions, of which the causal arrangement of the events produced is a faithful copy.

For all that, these clearly are actions, clearly are animated, though in less vivid a way, clearly are performances, though the relation of doing is now more tenuous, and are clearly appropriately related by 'in', 'by', 'in order'. My strategy is to give a very general account of the hierarchical organization of action, which makes best and clearest sense for cases resembling those I first described, but which has room in it for the others. In proceeding this way I am indirectly arguing for a claim about the application of the concept of action. I think that it primarily applies to cases in which the animation of the behaviour, its reflection of a hierarchy of desires and intentions in the groupings, phrasings, articulations of the agent's environment, is intuitively inescapable. It is from these, which I suspect it is part of human nature to recognize and respond to, that we understand the difference between acting and just moving or being acted on. And thus it is from these that we must begin to reconstruct a structure which may also contain all the other things that we more sophisticatedly call action.

To construe actions as I have been describing them, is to be committed to a model, very general and very permissive, but perfectly definite, of their production. One begins an action with a description of what one is generally intending to achieve. Then, while acting or preparing to act, one produces successively more detailed descriptions in response to the accumulation of information from the environment and in response to the need to co-ordinate one action with another. (These two are clearly closely related: the need for co-ordination, the possibility of interference between actions, is more evident the more specifically they are described, the more they are directed at the details of the environment.)

The central idea is thus that of an operation that can be applied over and over again, cyclically to its own results, of taking a description of an action, checking against the facts and coming up with more specific co-ordinated sub-actions. That is, we conceive of actions as organized according to the develop-

ment of the intentions that underlie them, and in this development specificity and co-ordination go together: an action as
described in an intention is developed into a set of more
specific component actions, which could be performed in
co-ordination, and each of which can be further developed. The
general form of the idea is familiar from grammar; rules that
generate strings from single items lead to tree structures in
which a node immediately dominates nodes labelled by the
members of the string that a rule generates from it. In the
case of actions, the 'rules' are the respecifications of intentions
and the nodes of the resulting tree are the intentions corresponding to co-ordinated descriptions of actions. (A glance forward
to the diagram on page 128 may help here.)

This may seem like an elaborated triviality. In a way it is,
since it is meant to be just what is in the very ordinary concept
of action. But it has some substantial consequences. It entails
that the co-ordination of actions can be construed by common
sense in only two ways. There can be pre-established harmony
or there can be causal interaction (occasionalism isn't allowed).
That is, actions that are traceable to some common node will in
performance be co-ordinated inasmuch as they will each have
inherited from the set of descriptions that emerged at that node
features which when realized ensure their fitting together when
performed. (For example tonguing a note and fingering it, both
further specifications of the intention to play it, presumably
occur at the same time because in setting oneself to do each
one has specified a time at which the movement is to be made.)
And then any two actions may be co-ordinated in that the
specification of each may mention conditions depending on the
performance of the other. (If one's description of tonguing the
note did not specify a common time for tonguing and fingering,
one could tongue when one felt one's fingers reach the right
position. It wouldn't work very well.)

Another, closely related, consequence of the model is that the
development of the action always proceeds downward; once a
description has been generated it is never changed. New
information has to be accommodated in the further specifica-

tion of the actions. (Imagine someone knitting, and moving the two needles in the usual co-ordinated way. Unexpectedly, a stitch begins to slip off the top of one needle. One takes the description of the action one was beginning, say to hold the left needle still and loop the wool from the right needle around to make another stitch, and modifies it so that while looping around with the right one also moves the left, to bring its tip further out.) In effect this creates a distinction between improvised remedies to a continuing course of action, and abandonments of that course of action in favour of another. While in practice this distinction does not seem very easy to apply, the principle behind it does seem to be part of common sense: we do not take a set of actions to be parts of a common course of action unless there is some common intention (which if realized specifies a larger action) of which they are both refinements. (In this connection see the Aside on transformations, below.)

ACTIONS AND INTENTIONS

The structures I have been describing are those that actions would have if they conformed perfectly to our intentions, and if our intentions evolved in a perfectly orderly manner. Notoriously, imperfection reigns over both planning and execution. Yet most things agents do have some relation to their intentions, and the structure of their actions is rather like that of their intentions. I think the facts are as follows.

One begins with desires, which become intentions to act by processes, call them 'practical reasoning' to give a name to the unknown, of enormous complexity. Then these intentions evolve, often in the development of a course of action, becoming more numerous and more specific in the way I have described. As a result, things happen, the environment changes, the body moves, and chains of effects ripple out into the world. I am not going to assume that there is any lowest level of intention and action where the two marvellously coincide, that there are any basic actions. I am not sure there are any; the scheme I am describing doesn't need them. (And, besides, if one believes they exist one finds oneself acting through that image, trying to control them, and it doesn't work; it's the disease of the over-conceptualizing agent.) Some of these resulting effects are describable as actions. They are distinguished in three ways.

First, there are those that result directly from the workings of the articulating processes. No doubt we actually recognize these as actions because of their intuitive, empathetic natural-ness; we can mentally dance along to them. More formally, they are those effects of one's intentions whose nature depends systematically on the articulation of one's intentions. Had one wanted to shape the music a little bit differently it would have got so shaped, differently. This does not require that they satisfy the propositional content of intentions. If one is painting a picture, and one's intention is to paint an accurate representa-tion of General Brock turning back the American invasion at Queenston Heights, then what one does is an action because it is controlled by one's intention in this way, even though the representation of the battle may be grotesque.

Second, there are those effects of one's intentions that, though they do not themselves *exhibit* the articulations of the intentions, are nevertheless results of the articulatedness of the agent's course of action. They are causally related to one another in patterns that depend on, among other things, the agent's attempts to shape the world, and which result in the realization of some of his desires. That is, they are parts of systems of events which have the form they do because of the agent's acting on his desires. (See the diagram on page 128.)

And third, there are those occurrences that, whether as a result of one's actions or of one's motions or just of one's presence, happen to satisfy one's intentions. What one had wanted to bring about comes to be. This is rarely enough all alone to qualify something as an action. We usually require some element of the first two characteristics. We tend towards the vocabulary of action, though, to describe types of event which are typically brought about as actions, especially when they conform to the agent's intention. Thus we say that someone did a perfect imitation of Groucho Marx, when he intended to, even though its perfection resulted more from the effect of the

THE KINDS OF ACTION

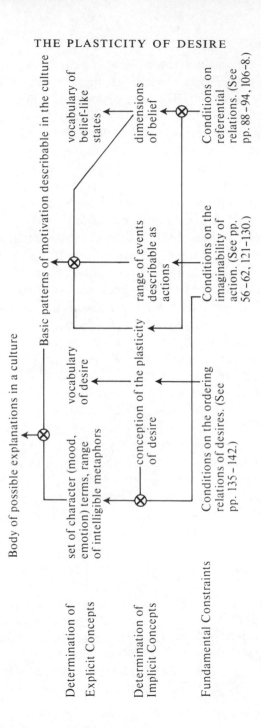

Body of possible explanations in a culture —— Basic patterns of motivation describable in the culture

vocabulary of belief-like states   dimensions of belief

Conditions on referential relations. (See pp. 88–94, 106–8.)

range of events describable as actions

Conditions on the imaginability of action. (See pp. 56–62, 121–130.)

set of character (mood, emotion) terms, range of intelligible metaphors   vocabulary of desire   conception of the plasticity of desire

Conditions on the ordering relations of desires. (See pp. 135–142.)

Determination of Explicit Concepts

Determination of Implicit Concepts

Fundamental Constraints

amount he had drunk, producing those rubbery knees and those rolling eyes, than from the workings of his intentions. We do so just because imitations are usually done as actions, usually intentionally in fact, and so we have the vocabulary handy, and would be hard pressed to describe the situation without it. When we have the resources, though, we make finer distinctions between action and non-action. Consider the fact that some people have control over the pitch and stress pattern of their voices and can control them (perhaps without knowing that that is what they are doing) for effect, and some other people cannot. We say of someone of the first kind 'she lowered her voice at this point, drawing attention away from the fact she had inadvertently revealed', and of someone of the second kind 'her voice faded away, lowered, as she said this, as she realized what she had just admitted'. The difference is subtle, and we only make it when there is some point to doing so, but what it amounts to is the difference between action and non-action.

These are three rather different ways in which happenings qualify as actions; there is a rather vague principle unifying them. Actions of all three kinds are consequences of the attempt by the agent to instantiate co-ordinated intentions; the attempt may not be successful, but what it results in tends to be action, for actions are those events which are shaped by the result of the attempt. Such an over-all definition of action has to be fuzzy, and philosophically frustrating, for we expand and contract the category of action at our convenience. We are not completely free in doing so, of course; actions have to be the sorts of things that we explain by reference to desires, beliefs, intentions. This makes the consequences of taking an event to be an action very substantial, I think; but it imposes only very vague restrictions on what we may try to extend the concept of action to.

ASIDE: TRANSFORMATIONS

The procedures that generate trees of action look much like phrase-structure grammars (or would if one expressed them with more rules, as e.g. theories of musical performance). So a natural question is: does one need transformations? A number of observations. First, a transformational structure is plausible in the articulation of many actions. That is, it seems intuitively right that we conceptualize them as possessing one hierarchical organization which has got transformed into another. For example, syncopation and other processes that rearrange parts of a rhythmic structure seem to be *intended* to be taken in this way. So (in 4/4 time)   could be derived as:

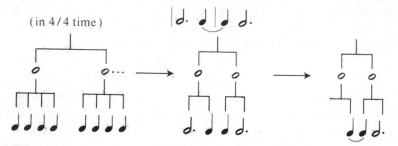

(For transformational structures in music see Peter Westergaard, *An Introduction to Tonal Theory* (Norton, New York, 1975).)

Mozart is very transformational. Second, it is formally very attractive to consider the adaptation one makes to an action description drawn from one's repertoire to fit it to particular circumstances as consisting of the application of transformations to a remembered tree-like 'deep structure'. This would tie the ideas of this chapter and those of Chapter II together very neatly. In general, in producing a new action to meet a new circumstance one would draw a *set* of action descriptions from the repertoire and apply suitable many–one transformations resulting in the desired performance. Third, and even less responsibly than the first two, the suggestion would seem to hint at an answer to the troubling question of how the language-specific apparatus that results in the transformations postulated in Chomskian linguistics could have arisen in human evolution. The answer hinted at is that transformations are something the hand taught the tongue; human manipulatory ability required that skills be variable in a way that required transformations, so that neurological processes came to be available which were later taken over in the production of speech. The transformation-providing machinery would then have undergone a final readaptation in finding a place in grammar. There is in fact a little rather ambiguous evidence of a connection between the development of manipulatory skills and the acquisition of language in children.

INTENTIONALITIES

Actions are things that happen in the world, and at the same time they are the objects of people's intentions. In particular the concept of intentional action poises what falls under it very delicately in between intention and effect; the same thing is what one intended to do and what resulted from one's trying to achieve one's intention. It is this balancing that interests me about intentional action, and which best brings out parts of my general theme. My aim here is to show how even in the case of intentional actions there is no simple congruence between the content of the intention and the nature of the achieved result. The idea that there is a natural class of actions which exhibit such a congruence arises, I think, out of simplistic views of moral responsibility and a Cartesian picture of will.

One wants something to happen and intends to bring it about, and then it happens; one may not have done it intentionally, if one has done it at all. It may happen in the wrong way, typically in a way that cuts across the way one had anticipated bringing it about. One means to shoot someone and then while getting set up to do it the pistol goes off by mistake. A number of writers have discussed examples like this to show how crucial the connection between intention and action is, and how much we require of this connection if the resulting action is to be intentional.[3] My plan is to continue this direction of argument until the original position gets turned more or less upside-down. I want the connection to become more central and definite than the intention, so that I can in the next section return to the role of desire in explanation freed of the assumption that in intentional action, presumably one of the main and most suitable objects of everyday psychology, there are always definite and formulable intentions.

Consider actions that take place over a period of time, as the environment and the agent's desire change. For example our oboist as he plays through to the end of the sonata, improvising a new interpretation of the last movement because of his misbehaving reed. Most intentional actions are to a greater or a lesser degree like this, they involve the assimilation of information that was not available when they were begun (sometimes

<hr />

[3] In this connection see Donald Davidson, 'Freedom to Act', in Ted Honderich, ed., *Essays on Freedom of Action* (Routledge and Kegan Paul, Boston, 1973); Roderick Chisholm, 'Freedom and Action', in K. Lehrer, ed., *Freedom and Determinism* (Random House, N.Y., 1966); and Chapter 3 of Goldman, op. cit.

the purpose of parts of the action is to uncover relevant information) and its use not only in the choice of the right means to a fixed end but in the choice of an end.

Such actions can be used as counter-examples to definitions of intentional action as the accordance of what happens with a plan formulated in advance, however elaborate it may be. One might well then modify the definitions, so that the plan may be formulated as the action proceeds, or as it is completed. It's a matter of ingenuity; perhaps it can be done. The main obstacle would be the fact that a plan formulated as the action developed could be always a moment behind the facts, reflecting rather than guiding them. Presumably some people's actions are like this: they have the illusion of being in control of things while actually they decide to bring something about only when it becomes inevitable. *Pace* Sartre, these actions aren't intentional.

In fact, the obvious inversion of the right causal order in such examples makes the problem seem easier rather than harder. For when the causal order is the right way round, we seem to have all we need. Take any unproblematic action, in which the parts unroll towards their end in an orderly adjustment to the environment: a cat stalking and leaping on a moving prey, a properly measured conversation, a chess game (taken from one side). The agent produces some effects, and some things just happen, and one of the shapes of the result can be traced to the step-by-step evolution of the agent's intentions. So we call the action intentional for three uncomplicated reasons. The causal roots of that shape of the event lie in the branchings of the agent's intentions, so they have that characteristic articulation; among the results of these articulated segments are events satisfying the more explicit and motivating of the agent's intentions; and the effect of all this is a significant enough part of the whole event that it makes sense to describe it and explain it as an action, as the result of the development of those intentions.

This gives, in effect, a definition of intentional action; it's at any rate definite enough to recognize a counter-example. And some kinds of counter-examples are immediate enough. The most popular philosophical examples of intentional action are not stretched-out series of things with the kind of articulation I am selling. One pulls a trigger, pushes a button, makes a signal, signs one's name, lets go a rope, and then it has to be determined whether the connection between the intention and the action is of the delicately correct kind necessary for intentional action. The connection is not out there to be seen in the action, as it is in the examples I have discussed (where it does not matter whether and how the little generating actions are intentional as long as the agent is reacting to and guiding the whole).

The actions we take to be intentional fall into two rough classes, I think. There are plans revealed during their evolution in time, of the kind I discussed. And then there are *voluntary* actions, in a more or less physiological sense of the word, actions which satisfy our intentions by the use of the standard physical processes, however it is that they work, through which we usually control what we do. So if one insists on a definition of intentional action one should say what I said above about extended actions and then add: there are also intentional actions produced by the processes that translate desire into movement in the following cases, giving a list of favourite examples of simple voluntary actions, such as those I produce in typing the letters of this page.

The grouping of these apparently disparate kinds of action together as intentional is not arbitrary, given an account of action which treats voluntary actions as resulting from a sort of miniaturization of the processes that guide extended controlled projects. Assumptions amounting to this are made by a style of explanation that has had a useful and influential history in our culture. It traces voluntary actions to acts of will, which result from particular single intentions through perseverance and mental directedness. (See the first of the explanations in the last section of Chapter II.) These assumptions are not made by universal psychological common sense, I'm sure, though my suspicion is also, probably unfashionably, that there is enough truth to them to make intentional actions into a rough natural kind.

Many things people do are likely therefore to be neither

intentional nor in any of the clear categories of the non-intentional. They are neither just successful articulations nor voluntary movements nor on the other hand mistakes, slips, actions from ignorance. Consider at one extreme a life's work. Darwin labours for fifty years and sets biology on its modern course. He does not do it by mistake, to be sure; he is lucky, though, and he uses the opportunities he finds, never knowing quite where he is going. He never meant to do *that*, anything like what he did; even at the end, dying, he need not have known what he had done or thought of it as something he would want to have done. There is a definite something, though, that is his accomplishment, and we can explain it as an action. And it is pointless to wonder whether it is intentional, accidental, or whatever; we are not short of useful things to say about it.

At the other extreme consider ejaculation: intended very often, planned, arranged, carefully set up. But neither articulated nor exactly voluntary. You can't dictate exact time and manner, nor is it produced by these usual unknown channels of nerve and muscle. The conformity of the act to the intention may be as good as in many standard pulling-the-trigger examples of intentional action, but still something is missing, atypical. The lack is clearly in the link between intention and action; the intention doesn't modulate the action; you set a bomb in your body, and another's, and then you can only indirectly affect the fuse. Intentional? Why should there be an answer?

The moral of these observations, for action and its explanation, is the fragility of the notion of intention. Actions are typically the result of states in the category of desire: wants, wishes, lusts, whims, and also intentions. Each of these has a specific characterizing role in the etiology of actions, but only of intention is it plausible that the action that results from the state is labelled by the same sentence as the state's content. When we see that this does not in general hold, and that even with intentional actions it is a pretty shaky principle, we may begin to look for more subtle and realistic relations between the characterization of an action and the content of the states that lead to it.

FREUD ON THE PLASTICITY OF DESIRE

Freud gave a new interest to something we had known all along, that desire is plastic, can assume new shapes according to the pressures and moulds around it. That refused love becomes hate (desire to join becomes desire to destroy) or that disciplined resentment becomes loyalty (desire to resist becomes desire to overcome the resistance of others) are commonplaces, if perennially puzzling. We know that these happen; we have little grasp of the laws by which they happen. Freud lessened the puzzle somewhat by showing us forms the laws could take. He provided a system of devices by which a desire is characterized, identified, not by its objects—these being relatively superficial and temporary possessions—but by *aims*. The aim of a desire is its role in the causation of action, best thought of as a very general specification of the kinds of situation it will accept as satisfying it.[4] Freud took the aims of desires to be the achievement of various pleasures. If we formulate things more abstractly than this, if we leave open what kinds of things the aims of desire ultimately are, we can avoid the, to me, implausible features of his theory of instinct, while maintaining the force of his suggestion that desire is the fundamental attribute of human beings. While rational agents all over the universe no doubt have beliefs and states of character, and also desires, in people, in our own species, it is desire that underlies these other states, that is malleable enough to be taken by us as the basic term in the laws of our nature.

Freud's account of desire arises out of the following basic difference between belief and desire. When one belief replaces another, generally the superseded one disappears, has no more effect on action, is a former state. But when one desire replaces another generally the superseded desire does not disappear but withdraws, awaiting a call or an opportunity to reappear. Of course it isn't always that simple; beliefs can linger and desires

[4] See 'Three Essays on the Theory of Sexuality', *Standard Edition of the Psychological Works of Sigmund Freud* (International Universities Press, vol. 7, 1964), and 'Instincts and their Vicissitudes' (*Standard Edition*, vol. 14).

can disappear. But before taking some of the reasons for this into account I want to connect the permanence of desire, as I have just simplistically formulated it, with the Freudian idea of its plasticity.

Desires are typically replaced with other desires because of strategic considerations; one decides or discovers either that one means is better than another for achieving an end, and so wants it instead, or that the satisfaction of one desire is incompatible with that of another, so that one and not the other may be maintained. In either case, one puts one desire into suspension. And in either case the change is motivated, there are reasons for it stemming from prior, more basic, desires. Take these more basic desires to persist after the shift of less basic ones, then, if conditions change or other considerations appear, the shift can be reversed and the displaced desire can return. The same return can happen with beliefs, of course. However, with desires there is a systematic structure to the shifts. If we arrange desires in an order, according to which are desired as means to the satisfaction of which others, we find that the shift of desire is roughly continuous along this ordering, that thwarted desire retreats down only as far as need be, and then when it can it filters up again.

As a result there is a great natural attractiveness to the idea that desire is like some plastic flowing substance that moves from basic to less basic positions. When one desire generates another then the new desire is invested with the motivational force of the original desire. The force of desire shifts around, from object to object. A formal representation of the concept of desire would thus be subject to the following constraints. With every agent at every time there would be associated a set of propositions, the potential objects of desire, and a relation between them, which I would expect to be at least a partial ordering (reflexive, transitive, antisymmetric). Then the specification of the agent's state of desire would consist of a set of *objects*, of propositions desired, and of a set of *aims*, of chains of propositions connected by the ordering relation. Objects and aims would be connected by the requirement that each object of desire be on some chain and that each chain consist of propositions that are objects of desire.

What is natural and commonsensical about the Freudian idea of the plasticity of desire seems to be captured by this, though of course it is also an attempt not to capture the whole content of the Freudian account. There are further requirements that it would be very natural to try to impose on the structure. For example, one would expect the chains of desire to converge 'downward', that there be a tendency for branchings to occur more often in one direction than another. It is hard to see exactly how to formulate this without saying too much.

It should be pretty clear that desires as we conceive of them commonsensically do have this dual semantics of aim and object, and that this is reflected in the nature of deliberation and action. In any case some consequences of the idea will be discussed in the next section. To characterize desires thus is, however, to say little more than that they do have a plastic motivational force. It is not to commit oneself to either of two further points. First, one is not committed to any view of the nature of the aims of desire. It may be that, as Freud argues, desires are organized into very extensive structures deriving their force and their aim ultimately from desires which we cannot consciously articulate and which are related to the satisfaction of instinctual drives. Formally speaking, this would entail that the ordering relation connect every object of desire ultimately with one or another of a small number of basic propositions, which are related to no other propositions by the ordering. This is clearly not the sort of thing that an analysis of the concept of desire ought to settle one way or another. Second, one is not committed to any view of the permanence or extensiveness of the structures in which desires are embedded. All that is part of the use of the concept of desire in everyday psychological explanation is that in attributing a desire to an agent in the context of explaining some particular action one indicates such a structure, from which the motivational force of the desire can be understood. How stable aad extensive such structures are is clearly a matter that will vary from one style of explanation to another, and about which the facts are not at all easy to ascertain. Any general formulation of our conceptions of desire will have to capture, as Freud's does, its most basic attribute, that it moves, that in action we find desires pushing and beliefs guiding. Desire can emerge as a *force* in Freud's psychology because of its plasticity, because like a physical force it can be directed, turned aside, re-routed, without losing its force. I cannot imagine how one could express this attribute of desire, its motive force, without in some way representing the duality of aim and object.

ASIDE: PLASTIC DESIRE AND SYMBOLICAL ACTION

It seems to me that Freud's psychology contains two important elements that are really rediscoveries of possibilities given by common sense and hidden by the rationalistic form educated common sense has often taken. The first is a full realization of the plasticity of desire. The other is a loosening of the relation between a desire and the situation that satisfies it, so that the satisfying condition can be a symbolical enactment of the desire. I think, moreover, that these two realizations are closely related. Three examples of their connection, first, dreams. It may seem an arbitrary stipulation that the latent content of a dream is always (always in his earlier writings, at any rate) a wish. Why not sometimes a belief? One very basic reason is that only a desire can get so turned round and changed and yet be itself, only a desire has an aim to identify it through its trans-mutations. Then there is the architecture of cathexes, of temporary stopping-places invested with the force of desire, which makes up the Freudian account of character. A situation or action that satisfies an articulate desire will also satisfy the system of cathexes that underlie the temporarily explicit form the desire has taken, and in relation to these underlying desires the satisfying condition must be more a symbolic realization than a logical instance, both because of the primitive nature of the conceptualization of such desires and because of the need simul-taneously to satisfy numbers of them via this improvised, shaky architec-ture. And lastly there is the 'acting out' of repressed desires in neurotic symptoms. Here the symbolic nature of the satisfaction of the desire is evident, but it seems completely inconceivable why the desire should accept this currency in payment for its demands (it wants parents kept from sleeping together and it gets a bolster placed in the middle of a child's bed) until one realizes that the repressed desire is itself a front for a complex of very primitive demands, in terms just of which the symbolic realization cannot be discriminated from a more literal one.

Freud rediscovered the connected notions of plasticity and of symbolic realization, and gave them back to us in the form of a theory which made very particular, uncommonsensical, claims about the ends of desire and the nature of symbolism. *Part* of the allegiance to psycho-analytic theory that many of us have derives from our gratitude at discovering that we could construct quasi-commonsensical explanations and feats of imagination that we would otherwise have thought impossible.

A VARIETY OF WANTINGS

The natural, commonsensical, element in Freud's account of desire is, if there is anything to what I have been saying, the insistence that the evolution, the dynamical process, by which desires create other desires and eventually result in actions, involves a corresponding evolution of the *content* of the desire, of what it is directed at and what it will accept as satisfying it. It isn't as if the desire says 'I want *that*', and then to satisfy it one has to produce just that. Rather, it says, 'I want something, and here's what it must do for me' and then one can search round offering it various things until something satisfies it. On Freud's application of this point, the relation between a desire and what satisfies it becomes one in which the satisfying conditions symbolize some one of a stratification of latent contents attached to the desire. And then the negotiation between desire and satisfying condition consists in the desire's managing to retreat or advance to a proposition which corresponds to the condition.

Certainly common sense does not commit us to anything like Freud's picture, attractive and powerful as it may be. But it does not restrict us, either, to taking desires to be essentially attached to particular contents, and to be satisfied only by the realization of these. If common sense were committed to this it would take the link between desire and action to be made of calculation: one wants a definite something and believes that something will get it for one, and so one brings this something about. Surely this is sometimes how belief and desire are tied to action. I take it that decision theory or utility theory amounts to an attempt to knit this tie into something capable of supporting a good proportion of the ways in which we act (reasonably, understandably) for what we want. My prejudice is to be suspicious of the attempt to capture in quantitative terms intuitions about the ordering of beliefs and desires, and of how these orderings lead to action, which are in their common-sensical origins of a structural rather than a quantitative nature. That is, I think that the ways in which one makes one desire defer to another, or lets a number of desires negotiate a mutually satisfactory disposition of the world, are accounted for in common sense in quite another way, which is closer to Freud's picture than to that of decision theory. The principles involved turn not so much on the relative *degrees* of belief and desire as on their *positions* in relation to their choice of object and their motivational force.

The best place to begin is with the array of concepts of desire: wish, want, lust, intend. . . . Their differences are as significant and as exploited as those between concepts in the category of belief. I can only discuss one system of contrasts between them: the difference in their specificities, and correlated with this the different strengths of attachment to their objects. Contrast two extremes: intention and wishing. One intends an action (or, sometimes, for something to happen under one's supervision) and this intention is connected to a fairly small range of possible actions as outcomes; if none of these occur the intention is just not satisfiable, and fades away (though wants that gave rise to it may not). On the other hand a wish, especially an idle wish, the wish of wishful thinking, has as object a very generally defined range of states of affairs, typically far from actualization, which if not attained remain wished for. Wishes are more patient and permanent than intentions. There is then an apparent correlation between the permanence of a motivational state and its distance from action.

(The patience of a state such as wishing has another side: insatiability, greed, best seen in states of lust or need. Somehow correlated to the variety of results which will satisfy such a state is a lack of finality to this satisfaction. Unlike intentions and to a greater degree than wants or aspirations, they usually come back for more. But to discuss this would be to expose another whole dimension along which states of desire are arranged.)

The correlation between permanence and distance from action is not fundamental, though. The basic connection is between the permanence of a state and the variety of states of affairs that will satisfy it. Intentions are very specific, only a particular narrow class of results will count as satisfying one, while wishes are less particular; not that a wish may not often be for something perfectly definite, but that its satisfaction could, typically, come just as well from a variety of other occurrences. There is a characteristically large and fuzzy range of propositions which if they come true will find the wish contented. Or, to put the point differently, the identity of a particular wish depends more on its position with respect to other states of desire—which ones it is a further expression of, which ones would take up its force in the presence of various kinds of frustrations, which intentions it ultimately motivates— than on its propositional content. The content is indeed a real part of the wish, but the wish has that content as a result of other more essential attributes.

A different aspect of these contrasts comes from considering the fate of frustrated or overruled desires. One often does nothing to achieve something one wants, sometimes desperately wants, because of the incompatibility of satisfaction of that want, given the way the world is, with other more important (strong, pressing) wants. And any working motivational scheme will recognize the fact that much of what we do is due to the presence of these overruled desires. Their effect is obviously not through what we do to make their contents actual; it is less direct and less 'rational'. Most simply and understandably, one may find one's actions on the 'victorious' belief reluctant or feeble; one may be grumpy; one may *express* one's mixed feelings in no end of ways. With their ignorant accuracy, informal modes of explanation recognize with respect to non-dominant desires three terribly basic facts. Among the results of a desire there are very often none that are even intended to correspond to the propositional content we may use to describe it. The satisfaction of a desire by a situation is consequently a process requiring a more varied and delicate congruence of the one to the other. And in order to take care of these subtle congruences, we need a vocabulary that can express the different kinds of attachments that motivational states can have to their objects.

These three facts hold of the connections between dominant desires and action, too. I am convinced that there is no very crucial difference between dominant and non-dominant desires, either in point of fact or in everyday psychological explanation. And it is around this point that the different issues of this chapter come together. For in the hierarchical organization of desires and intentions that I found to be implicit in the structure of actions it is the less permanent and more particular states, the intentions to very specific acts, that occupy the lower (dominated) nodes and are directly connected to physical actions. The connections with action of states at higher levels in the tree-structures are less direct and consist less of direct instantiation; they are better described as wants than as intentions. Similarly, the analysis of intentional action was meant to show how tenuous the connection is between the actions that may be expected to result from a desire and the proposition with which we label the desire, how it is not in terms of this that we call actions intentional; this conclusion is then given a new grounding in terms of the plasticity of desire; it turns out to be only in the nature of a very special class of desires that their propositional contents be more than temporary, almost accidental, attachments.

What one might expect me to do at this point, then, is to formulate a very general range of ways in which these two structures, the hierarchical organization in terms of which we articulate actions and the plastic architecture that we appeal to in laying out someone's motivation, may be connected, perhaps even derive them both from a single, more basic idea. And then different specific forms of these structures and their connections would constitute the different underlying conceptions of motivation at the heart of different styles of informal psychological explanation. I would love to be able to do this, but I cannot.

Instead, I shall work through an example in some detail. I

mean the example to be a quite ordinary case of explanation by motive, and I mean my discussion of it to bring out how varied the comparisons of desire and satisfying fact countenanced by common sense in such explanations are.

The agent manipulates a ball of clay in his hands, shaping it into a portrait-head of his father. His fingers push little indentations in and squeeze little folds out; he twists his thumb while pushing the side of its tip into the clay pressed against the palm of his other hand at first and later balanced between the tips of its fingers; he slides either index finger down the sides of the clay to draw out folds which the thumb of the other hand can shape as they emerge, into twisting ridges and flaps. He inserts the fingernails of his index and third fingers into the almost finished head, to make sharp lines for eyelids, lips, ear-lobes, and with his thumbs smoothes behind the work of his nails. As the head takes its final recognizable form, he holds it gently and gives the nose a friendly, but disfiguring, tweak.

Here is an idiomatic explanation of it. He had the clay in his hands by chance, and noticed a bump in it resembling rather his father's straight wide nose, and, turning it round in the light to see the 'nose' better, found his hands shaping cheeks and brow to frame it. He soon found that in pressing one feature onto the clay he would obliterate another he had previously formed, and so he worked systematically, first shaping the whole head and then drawing out the particular features while holding his fingers so as to minimize the pressure on what he had already done. The emerging head looked at him with just that mixture of insight and intolerance that he had always found in his father's gaze. And looking back at it and saying to himself 'well, you don't trouble me now', he took between his fingers the nose that had first attracted his eye and with aggressive forgiveness made the head ugly.

First strand of explanation: technique. He had in mind the appearance he wanted the clay to assume. He wanted his fingers to depress and draw out without crushing so he worked them in pairs, each balancing the push of the other and allowing the hand holding the clay steady not to inflict any deforming pressure. Working this way he worked each developing feature in constant comparison with an initially vague and steadily focusing image of what the head was to look like. When this image had become, as intention and as developing sculpture, definite enough to be disturbing, he changed it in the same way as he had made it, without affecting its general resemblance.

Notes on the first strand: The action is represented as the realization of a series of intentions, evolving in accordance with the accumulation of information about their effects. The intentions are specified in terms of the effects that follow from them, as intentions to move these fingers, to draw out this fold without crushing this protuberance, etc. The evolution of intentions centres on a comparison of the effect achieved up to the point in question with the plan at that point; both plan and intention are then respecified.

Second strand of explanation: means and ends. He wanted to make a model of his father's head, and the best way of doing this was to let his fingers work over the clay until it began to look right, for he had managed in the past to get good likenesses this way and he knew that if he tried to proceed with too definite an image before him or too fixed an idea of what each manipulation of the clay was to become he would be less likely to get his result. Then when the head was just about finished he just followed the last disfiguring turn the shape he was aiming at took, and accomplished it in the same reliable way.

Notes on the second strand: the intentions are articulate, they can be stated in terms of their content even if their content is not realized. The development of these intentions is largely a matter of practical reasoning, carried out in isolation from the performance of any action, at the heart of it is a comparison of the results of possible courses of action with an underlying intention. This comparison results in the selection of 'dominated' intentions to action and the evolution, usually in the direction of greater specificity, of the 'dominating' intentions.

Third strand of explanation: symbolism. First of all he had wanted to make his father appear, after the 'nose' in the clay had brought a whole set of thoughts to mind. As he worked on the clay, thoughts of his father naturally occurred to him as he produced those features with their various meanings. At the end of working with the clay he had worked his thoughts about his father to a point of feeling his desire to harm him, and of understanding the harmlessness of wanting this. And so, as an expression of this desire and this realization, he attacked the head he had made.

Notes on the third strand: The intentions here are not realized; their satisfaction consists in their being expressed. This expression occurs when the results of the action, as perceived by the agent, bear a rather abstract resemblance to the content of the intention. Intentions of this sort are satisfied by a very loose comparison with the results of action. And how could it be otherwise? For the intentions are so far removed from the objects whose presence originally made them and occupy such a basic position in the hierarchy of desires that the detailed set of intermediate intentions that would be needed to connect their specific content with a literal realization cannot occur.

These three strands of explanation are quite compatible with one another, and all can be parts of a wider explanation of the action. Each could be produced alone, however, and be an adequate, if not terribly comprehensive, explanation. And someone who produced one of them could find another of them unintelligible or uninformative, especially if the way in which he would expand his favoured explanation to account for the features explained by the others would proceed by an extension of its characteristic level of intention and mode of comparison of intention and result. Each of the strands of explanation I have separated out is also an expression of a general style of explanation-by-desire, a general way of extracting intentions from desires and of comparing these with the situations which satisfy them.

I do not think that there is any *a priori* limit to the variety of such styles of explanation. The 'universal' features seem to be as follows. There are three inevitable components of any scheme of explanation by desire. First one has a specification of the permissible descriptions of a set of motivational states (e.g. intentions to manipulate objects, described in terms of the manipulations that result, desires or intentions to perform particular actions, wishes with a content distinct from the objects of action). Then one has a specification of the ways in which a partial achievement, as perceived or otherwise discovered, can be compared with one of these states, resulting in one or more of: the generation of a more specific intention to carry on or carry out the act; the respecification of the state in question, typically resulting in its becoming closer to the details of what has been revealed as attainable; or lastly the abandonment of the whole idea, possibly in favour of some alternative. And as the third component one has a set of restrictions on the ordering of the structure of desires, as discussed in the Freud section; these specify general 'algebraic' properties of its ordering, the position of various particular types of desire in it, and the relative specificity of these types of desire.

I am making two claims. One is that any common-sense style of psychological explanation that describes actions as the result of the interaction of beliefs and desires—and I suspect further that any adequate style of explanation must have some part doing this—will produce explanations that can be represented along these lines. The other is that any systematic pattern of explanation that satisfies my requirements could be used under suitable circumstances as a common-sense mode of explanation and understanding. We could learn to produce the explanations and to imagine the actions through them. By 'suitable circumstances' I mean an environment of causal processes which reflect the structures of intentions given by the explanations in the causal articulation of the actions explained. In other words, if a scheme satisfying these requirements works, if it allows us to take its explananda as actions, then we could use it.

Explanations which construe an action as rational, in the tradition of Aristotle or Hobbes, are a special case of explanation by motive. Any analysis of rational action will suggest ways of comparing a possible course of action with the desired end and judging it acceptable or unacceptable. A number of bases for such comparisons have been suggested, involving maximizations of various quantities between competing possible actions. No doubt some are more suitable than others for use in various circumstances, given the sort of world we think this is, but answers to these questions may not help delimit the variety of such comparisons found in common-sense styles of explanation. Completely different ways of conceiving the relation between an intention and its satisfaction, for example via the kind of symbolical realization found in the third strand of the explanation above, taken to great lengths in psycho-analysis and not at all uncommon in common-sense explanation, may be at least as central to perfectly natural understandings of mind, and may in fact be just as near to the real psychological facts, whatever they are. To focus too exclusively on calculating rationality is to see only one very particular aspect of our capacities to imagine why we act. It is, I suspect, part of a general blindness that we easily fall into, which makes us also take intentional actions as the paradigmatic examples of the intelligible in what we do and makes us susceptible to what in the last chapter I called the myth of belief. Whether or not all these things are more than accidentally connected, to take maximization, intentional action, or belief as central to our understanding of mind is unnecessary and, in a very definite way, parochial.

VI

CHARACTERS

> Susan Shepherd's word for her, again and again, was that she
> was 'large'; yet it was not exactly a case, as to the soul, of
> echoing chambers: she might have been likened rather to a
> capacious receptacle, originally perhaps loose, but now drawn
> as tightly as possible over its accumulated contents . . . Mrs
> Lowder . . . was spacious because she was full, because she had
> something in common, even in repose, with a projectile, of
> great size, loaded and ready for use.
>
> Henry James, *The Wings of the Dove*

CHARACTERS AS UNITS

We explain people's actions by referring to the play of beliefs
and desires, to the influence of other propositional states, and
to various specifiable dispositions to action. These, together
with the situations of agents in their surroundings, are the
essential elements of psychological explanation; they are what
we explicitly mention. The reasons why one *believes* an explanation to be correct, or the basis on which one forms an expectation about a future action, however, are very often quite
different. They can consist in apprehensions of a kind that one
finds enormously hard to articulate, about the mood and
character of the person in question. When we are able to
express these judgements of what people are like, we are likely
to do it indirectly, by use of metaphor, by comparison of one
person with another, or by describing consequences of people's
mood, character, or emotion for what they may think or do.

One says of someone 'she drove to Winnipeg in the snow-
storm to see the ballet'. And then to explain why this desire
would make her risk her life, one says 'she's deprived of
anything cultural, out there in Brandon, and she's determined,
it's part of her self-respect that she will do such things'. To show
how the explanation applies one talks of mood and character.

But this talk does not go very far. '*I*'m just as interested in the arts, and it is as much a part of my self-respect to act on this interest, but you'll not catch me in a snow-bound car at forty below because of a recital.' So one tries to express the particularities of the case. 'Her commitment is less confident than yours, she has to keep affirming it, and then it's as if this affirmation makes the commitment seem hollow and so she acts very uncomplicatedly from it, to sort of cover up her motives with a simple surface.' She appears to deceive herself into straightforwardness. And if even this does not get across the difference between her and the other, then the description of character gets longer, less explicit, and more exact.

One might suspect then that the *content* of these judgements when there is something definite enough to be called that, consists essentially of bundles of expectations about what the person in question will do, think, feel. They would be so hard to express, then, because of the difficulty of giving in a few words the sense of a whole pattern of thought or action. I don't think that this is quite right; I shall argue that one's understanding of what particular people are like can be less closely tied to one's expectations of their states and actions. It consists, *very* roughly, of what one would have to know in order to begin imagining how they do what they do.

It is clear enough why one might want to hold some such view given an emphasis such as mine in Chapter III on the role of the imagination in psychological explanation. For if we learn anything by imagining what people are like and what lies behind their actions, it is clear from our fragmented reports of what we imagine that we do not express what we learn easily and do not connect it readily with what we expect people to do. I think, though, that the position can be argued from a more neutral starting point. Any view of psychological explanation will have to deal with the fact that often one can ascribe beliefs, desires, emotions to someone, correctly, and there can be a perfectly natural explanatory connection between these and some action of the person, which *might* therefore be explained by these states, and yet—they don't explain it, they don't tell why he did it. To know that an explanation applies is to know something beyond the truth of its premises and the reasonableness of its form. This is surely true, in different ways, for explanations of all sorts; the way I shall describe it with respect to psychological explanation connects it with a quite different class of phenomena. It is the existence of experiences like the following. Sometimes one has some idea what it is like to be someone else, in a particular situation or as the person he is. Sometimes one can imagine what a large part of someone's experience is like. And sometimes one takes a person, a whole personality, as the object of an attitude, notably love or hate which cannot be an attitude towards the person as characterized by all his easily attributable characteristics. (Someone could exhibit all of those, and one could be quite indifferent.)

All these disparate things, united on the surface only by the fact that it is easy to say foolish things of all of them, are manifestations of a single kind of knowledge, usually tacit, of personality. The basic point to argue is that what one needs to know in order to know that a psychological explanation applies, and the knowledge one has in various kinds of grasping of personality, are of a piece, fundamentally the same. It is quite evident, I suppose, that one acquires a lot of information about people that one cannot categorize simply as beliefs, desires, emotions, or any of the other familiar terms of the explanatory vocabulary. It is also not exactly heretical to point out that much of this information guides one's judgements of when a psychological explanation is to apply and is relevant to one's intuitions of the feel of a person's situation. What I must claim, to bring these two uses together, is that there is a common form, a standard conceptualization, that the information used for both purposes must take. The description of this standard form is the task of the rest of the chapter.

EXAMPLE: DEPTH OF CHARACTER

One says of people that they have hidden depths or that the apparent depth of their feeling is illusory, or that some particular part of their character, perhaps their loyalty to some ideal, is deep. To say just this would be banal and uninformative, so one usually decorates the image, to fit the particular person. The made-to-order metaphors one then comes up with are still governed by a general understanding of how the image of depth works. Deep is persistent; it is down where passing changes do not get at it. So deep motivation is stubborn, and tends to underlie more fluctuating desires. Deep is hidden, too, away from the surface of sociality. So deep thoughts and attitudes may be hard to express, and may evolve in ways that are hidden and hard to explain.

What is the use of describing through these images? One use is to serve as a corrective to more explicit description. A story: *A* says of *B*, 'It's pretty clear why she ditched George; his influence was no longer any use to her, and there was Simon, with all those stories and friends she could weave into her work.' And *C* denies the explanation, without denying the attributions, saying, 'No, she is as opportunistic as you think, and she does use her friends like that, but in a deeper way; she starts her thinking at the very bottom level with reactions to her friends and to their reactions to their friends, and I suppose the thing with George has dried up to the point where it can give her only anecdotes, and not these basic reworkable intuitions. But if she then replaced him with Simon it wasn't because of the number and influence of Simon's friends but because he is tied to them in such interesting, peculiar ways.' *C* would have difficulty making this comment without the image of deeper and shallower levels of *B*'s use of people. *C* is denying no attribution that *B* is making of *A*, but *C* is denying the explanation *B* makes of *A*'s actions. If one knows which of all the formally correct possible explanations actually does say why someone did something, one knows a pretty basic fact about what that person is like. To express, and think out, these basic facts of people's particular natures we need a vocabulary which cuts across the usual vocabulary of psychological explanation, which can select those particular explanations which apply to a particular person. It is for this reason that we have our highly improvisational vocabulary of character, mood, and emotion.

The understanding we get from using this vocabulary is shaped by its function. There is always a reference to more standard patterns of explanation. We conceptualize traits of character in terms of what our explanatory resources need in order to be true of individual cases. Thus, Simon in loving *B* focuses on the depth of her appreciation of her friends' sociality, glossing over the subtle exploitation this involves; he grasps this trait in her by understanding, for example, why 'she likes him because she can use his experience' is as it stands a misleading explanation of *B*'s befriending someone, and understanding how it can be expanded to be part of a more accurate explanation. In taking a personality, rather than a set of unconnected attributes, as the object of one's attitudes, one is seeing how the attributes can and can not be used in explaining the actions of the person.

THE INVENTION OF PERSONALITY

There are far less problematic impressions of personality, that take the form of explicit, literally expressible, beliefs that someone's character or mood is of some determinate sort. We think of people as hasty, kind, stupid, frantic, and we qualify our expectations of what they may do accordingly. And there is nothing notably metaphorical about most uses of these terms. If we could make do with just these descriptions we wouldn't have to have any dealings with diffuse images or inarticulate impressions. I think, though, that the two are inextricably connected, that one cannot use concepts of character, mood, or emotion without acknowledging that what one is trying to do with them may sometimes require less tidy attributions.

The function of concepts of character in psychological explanation is, as I indicated, to block, qualify, or emphasize the connections between the beliefs and desires that an explanation appeals to and the actions it explains. The idea is essentially that the use of these concepts has an overriding aim, that of fitting general patterns of explanation to the quirks of the particular case. This makes them inevitably quirky themselves: irregular, resenting regimentation. The first point to make is their resistance to being characterized in behavioural terms.

The point is this: if a character term, say 'haste', characteristically serves to pick out a class of intentions from which the person to which it applies may act (e.g. haste rules out the motives for double-checking what one does, and reinforces the motives of speed and efficiency), then the range of *actions* in whose explanation it can figure may not have any simple unity at all. The range of actions associated with such a term may in fact not characterize the term at all; they may, for example, be the same as the actions associable with some other term. Perhaps every action that can be done from haste can be done from care, and vice versa, given suitable variations in the accompanying beliefs and desires.

The difficulty is familiar enough in its general form; behavioural characterizations of psychological terms run foul of the fact that it is complexes of states rather than individual states that lie behind action. The position of terms of character in the connection of complexes of states with actions is rather special. Their purpose is not to be simply states among the other states which motivate action, but to operate at another level, as indicators of which complexes actually will connect with which actions. The ultimate perfect character term would thus give a paradoxical behavioural quality to the whole scheme. A set of states S and the term t would jointly hold only when one of a defining range of actions was performed, and given an action there would be a set of combinations of S and t which could account for it. This is impossible; at any rate it is beyond the wildest dreams of the kind of explaining we actually do. What we seem to do, in practice, is to use fixed patterns of explanation in terms of beliefs, desires, and other well-behaved states, which gets us as near as we can to this ultimate end, and then to let free use of the 'holes' left in these patterns for attributions of character (mood, emotion) take up as much of the slack as they can.

The result is clearly very imperfect. To have the concept of a character concept, though, is to share something of its hopeless aim; one wants to be able to capture in one's ascriptions of character the reasons why this particular person, at this time, is moved by these motives. And so we invent a labyrinth of character terms, interacting in their effects and stratified in complicated ways, to capture more and more of the particularity of people.

To understand about character concepts must be, then, to have mastered much of the concept of mind of socialized adults in one's culture. Here is a very schematic picture of a possible sequence of stages by which these concepts might be acquired.

To begin one has a crude grasp of the more literal terms of character and mood. At this stage they may be understood in terms of characteristic patterns of behaviour. Angry people curse and kick and move abruptly; sad people move slowly, don't notice much, and cry. A child who understands these as their meanings is on the right track. These can coexist with a grasp, at this stage more a simple skill than any kind of knowledge, of the modulability of one's own perception and behaviour, and of other people's styles of action, of a kind that is revealed in childish mimicry. There is no very evident connection between these things at this stage. Nothing here tells one what someone else's sorrow or anger is like (or one's own for that matter), and nothing generates the idea of a thing, experience, which both one and others have.

And then one bright day, one bright year perhaps, hitherto unintelligible parts of the culture begin to make sense as an awareness of the more subtle algebra of psychological explanation combines with a more developed knowledge of the facts of consciousness and of imitation; one realizes that the elements of the first stage are not unrelated. Most importantly, the two ineffabilities, ineffable in part because they were not at all propositional, those of the control of one's own manner of behaviour and those of others' individual styles, connect, via the connections each has with the application in terms of character.

Several things have to fit into place for this transition to occur. The simplest of them is just the correlation of terms of character with styles both of one's own and of other people's actions. One needs to have made this correlation in order, for example, to act according to adverbial instructions ('do it more carefully') or to fake an emotion one does not have (knowing what emotion it is one is faking). I would imagine this element to be prepared for by one's becoming aware of the same factors in the control of one's own behaviour and in one's imitation of others'. A considerably more subtle element is the realization of the variety of explanatory patterns that the culture affords one. One learns that one has to pick the right one for a particular person at a time, and one learns that, within very imprecisely set limits, one can play variations on standard forms of explanation to make them fit particular cases. And one learns that terms of character indicate some of these modulations of explanation. I imagine that a crucial step towards this is the understanding of the role terms of character play within the allowable patterns of explanation.

A final, consolidating, element is the discovery that one can partially represent the ways people seem to one and the ways one is trying to act, in terms of the classes of explanations that would be appropriate, and thus eventually in terms of traits of mood and character. A result of the consolidation, and a test of its having occurred, is the arrangement of character concepts in dimensional schemes of the kind social psychologists uncover. Such schemes can have little intelligibility to a purely behavioural understanding of character terms. Presumably they reflect the ordering of character concepts induced by underlying models of mind, which are most naturally studied in terms of the explanatory patterns in which the character concepts eventually find their home.

METAPHORS AND EXPLANATIONS

One test of the way one has come along this route, the sophistication one has acquired, is the use one makes of metaphor as a glue to hold together structured explanations, graspings of character, and management of oneself. The metaphorical devices we use here have various degrees of sophistication.

One device, not a very profound one, that we use to pick out a range of explanations appropriate to a particular person, is to

project a characteristic of some of the person's actions into a
feature of their personality. So we describe people as clumsy,
hasty, meticulous, abrupt, and use these labels to justify our
explanations of actions that are not themselves clumsy, hasty,
meticulous, or abrupt. What one is saying in describing a person
as abrupt is, roughly, 'think of an action performed abruptly,
imagine what it takes to act that way, and now keep this
imagined state in mind while thinking what one might do in
the following situation . . .'. With the right characteristics of
action to project, and the right unobtrusiveness at insinuating
them beyond their area of literal application, the trick works.
We get some increase in understanding of what people are likely
to do and what their motives may be.

A rather more subtle device, also for projecting from a class
of actions to a class of explanations is to construe the deliberation, practical reasoning, motivational process, whatever it is
that one takes to lie behind action, in terms of the same concepts
that one applies to action. In effect, one describes deliberation
as covert action. We say of someone that their delicacy is
pervasive, that their thinking is like the manipulation of some
fragile material which breaks if one bends it too quickly or ties
it too tight, or that the movement of their desire is like the
response of a creature made of glass, breakable both by resis-
ance to the forces on it and by a too abrupt response to
them.

There is something evidently mechanical about these action-
to-attribute and action-to-motivation projections. No such easy
picture of what is going on will lay out any of the really fine and
powerful metaphors. Often, as when we use one of the images
of depth, construing the mind as a nested system of fields of
action or as concentric shells of the permanence of desire, the
use we make of the image or model we produce is so delicately
embedded in the context of description and in the details of the
explanation being challenged, endorsed, or qualified, that just
stating some general pattern that it conforms to will miss the
force that it has in the particular case.

The metaphors of depth have a particular versatility, I think.

On different occasions they can introduce combinations of a great variety of considerations into psychological explanations. Let me mention five. (a) There is the difference in permanence and changeability between superficial and profound motives and beliefs, and roughly correlated with this the different intelligibilities of different beliefs. The metaphor presupposes that more permanent, 'deep-seated' states will be harder to state and less confidently ascribed. (b) There is the fact that thought is as much effect as it is cause, that thinking like action results from other thinking and from other states of the person. And so we try to represent thought as action, with its own field of action and its own mechanisms of articulation and execution. Inevitably, the result is that we conjure up a stratification of fields of action, since thoughts-as-actions are produced by further thoughts-as-actions, and so on, with each level having its own field of action. (c) We use the same style of imagery often to represent the different degrees of social accessibility or directness that different degrees of social accessibility or directness that different people exhibit at different times. Complicated social attitudes and motives are assimilated to the sketch of a pretentious person with layers and layers of make-up, clothes, wigs, and medals, presenting a persona defined only by the social significance of the show.

The usefulness of images of stratification and depth is increased also by their natural congruence with other metaphorical schemes, which are not based on literally spatial imagery. (d) We speak of thoughts and thinkings as being wounds and woundings, searches and hidings, attacks and protections, describing them in terms of physical actions. It is significant in comparison with (b) that we do this most readily when the action to which the thought is assimilated is one whose domain is spatial. (e) We describe processes of deliberation and decision as if they were the play of opposing teams of subsidiary selves. We speak of debates and struggles in the head and heart. Sometimes the selves or teams occupy loci in the space of their struggle; sometimes their opposition is less embodied, and the positions and resolutions themselves are formed into strata and hierarchies.

In any particular case one can combine implications of all these kinds. The sense one intends one's ascription to have, and the sense it is taken to have, is determined not only by the details of the image one presents and of the context in which one presents it, but also by the structure of the explanation at issue. Spatial imagery construed as with (a) can support the attribution of motives at apparent odds with an evident pattern of action; (b) can serve to motivate the application of blocking considerations, reasons why a motive did not have the effect one might have otherwise supposed it to have; (c) allows one to appeal to a whole underwear of motives hidden beneath a conventional appearance, and to describe that appearance itself as a set of motives; (d) provides a vocabulary for describing processes that would otherwise be hard to capture in the over-all scheme of motive, belief, and attempt; and (e) allows one to use inconsistent sets of beliefs and desires, suitably partitioned, to explain the details of a series of actions.

THE UNITY OF CHARACTER CONCEPTS

If I make some assumptions explicit, the unity that I have been claiming for knowledge of character may be clearer. Different styles of psychological explanation vary, I think, primarily in the use they make of terms in the category of belief and desire and in the ways they describe action. If there is a universal taxonomy of explanatory schemes, then it will come from pushing considerations like those of the last chapter rather than those of this one. Given the core of an explanatory scheme, a characteristic way of construing motivation and deliberation, there are no doubt many ways of adding on qualifications of mood and character. I expect, though, that the basic features of this core will determine what categories of character term can be added on to it. If we want to be able to say completely new things about emotions or characters, then we will probably have to find new ways of talking about motivation.

The only reason for believing these assumptions is that they have been implicit in the discussion so far, which has not resulted in any too glaring absurdities. Given the assumptions, though, we are provided with a theory of the way in which one's knowledge of things in the category of character is organized. One has available to one a range of basic explanatory patterns, and one has a vocabulary of terms of character, mood, emotion, each subcategory of which contains terms playing a particular role in qualifying the basic explanatory patterns. The actual vocabulary obviously does not cover all the states of mood or character one can imagine, attribute, or describe. If the vocabulary was adequate we would not need all the indirect devices, the metaphors and story-tellings, that I have described. But when one uses such a device what one is doing is in effect to define a new term, in an existing subcategory, to fit a pre-existing possibility.

For example: one says of someone 'he's not exactly lazy; he *feels* lazy at times and dreads the thought of getting out and doing anything, but he then acts as diligently as you could want; it is as if he can turn on his inertia as a fulcrum and really push an action with it beneath him'. The metaphorical last part would need to be elaborated before its sense came through clearly, but the direction of the whole thing is evident. It is an attempt to define a disposition to an emotion which is felt like laziness and has some of the same consequences for the way one plans one's future, but affects one's actions in a quite different way. Now laziness is not an emotion; it is a trait of character and sometimes a mood. There could be emotions which affected people in some of the ways that laziness does; such an emotion is being attributed to the person in the example. The general situation of the example seems to be somewhat as follows. We arrange concepts of character and the like in terms of their permanence, character being a pretty permanent business which does not change readily or easily and moods and emotions being transient. And we also arrange them in terms of the extent to which they change the agent's desires; character traits and emotions make one want what one would not otherwise, and moods leave one's wants largely unchanged and affect instead the actions one performs for these wants. I should add that I think that the tags 'character', 'mood', 'emotion' do not capture these distinctions very well; I think that the distinctions are part of the explanatory system in use around me, and I would like to be able to capture them better. Laziness, then, is as a long-term trait an element of character and can affect what one wants and as a short-term trait, as when one is just in a lazy mood, is a mood that affects motivation quite superficially. What is being attributed to our agent is something that is transient like the mood of laziness but affects motivation as involvedly as the character trait of laziness, but differently. And for lack of a word for it we have to become so cumbersomely expressive.

But what is to prevent one from just imagining someone possessing a trait that fits no slot in any pattern of explanation? Quite a lot. To begin one has to imagine a *person* having this trait, and thus the trait operating in conjunction with beliefs, desires, memories, perceptions. One has to have some handle on what possession of the trait will lead a person to do, and so one has somehow to reconcile the effect of the imagined trait with that of all these other factors. I cannot conceive how this can be accomplished except by using a pattern of explanation, or by cultural heroism inventing one, which fits the trait together with whatever other states are a necessary part of imagining a person's condition.[1]

---

[1] In the psycho-analytic literature one finds evocative descriptions of the ability to internalize or incorporate a personality. And one gets the impression that some primitive capacity to grasp the nature of another and hold it within one is being described, which is unconnected with the explanations or expectations one has of the other. Recent writings, however, seem to retreat from this, and emphasize instead the variety of kinds of internalization that can under different conditions take place. There is then no single phenomenon to consider; neither Freud's internalization of a whole personality-as-perceived nor Klein's symbolic incorporation of parts of a person-as-body will be anything like the whole story. See Roy Schafer, *Aspects of Internalization* (International Universities Press, New York, 1968). I may have no quarrel with this tradition, then. I certainly have no quarrel with the descriptions of how strong one's impression of what someone is like can be, and how hard it can be to express. In a variation on a draft of this chapter, called 'Character and Emotion' to appear in Amelie Rorty, ed., *Explaining Emotion* (University of California Press, Berkeley, 1979), I pay particular attention to the connection between the inexpressibility of some intuitions of personality and the existence of real facts for these intuitions to correspond to.

THE REALITY OF EXPLANATIONS

The attempt to give a systematic commentary on our explanations, to spell out the conditions under which they will succeed
and to adapt them to these conditions, is by its very nature a
business with few fixed rules. One takes the motives that are
claimed to underlie the action, and one tries to be as exact as
one can about the relations they may have to the facts of the
case. Sometimes one can work one's commentary into and
around the explanation, treating personality like character,
mood, and emotion; we have formal devices for doing this.
Sometimes one cannot, and there are occasions when all one
can do is endorse or deny the explanation, appealing to one's
authority as someone who knows the agent.

It is also by its nature a business that must often fail. For the
facts, the real psychological facts, about an agent's state of mind
and relation to the surroundings, are what makes an explanation
apply. A scattered set of true ascriptions of beliefs and desires
can rarely be expected to capture enough of these facts, even
when these beliefs and these desires are in some other person
responsible for a similar action. And mechanical ways of
working in attributions of character, mood, and emotion are
not always going to suffice to summon the particularity of
people. We can continually find ways of capturing further facts,
though, by inventing subtler patterns of explanation or by
managing to express further traits of character.

But however ingenious we are, it seems certain that the
dialectic continues, that as formal explanation becomes more
subtle further regions of intuition of personality become
available, as inexplicitly conceptualized, tacit, knowledge. The
inexpressible is always one step ahead.

This might be a disappointing fact if one were to expect that
our modes of psychological explanation could ever be completely autonomous, working according to stated general laws
from literally construed ascriptions. The fact that this is not so
is reassuring, though, if one's concern is with the reality of the
explanations that we use. One might worry that the standard

forms of psychological explanation that our culture affords us provide rationalizations rather than real explanations, that they allow one just to weave some words around an action so as to make it seem unsurprising, rather than in any more substantial sense explaining why it happened. Explanation is *not* always merely formal. We can be fairly sure of it because of the presence of concepts, of emotion, mood, character, whose main function is to force a general pattern of explanation to confront the details of each particular case. The presupposition in their use is that there are underlying facts of mental life, and that in any way we can we must connect what we say about people to these facts. Our successes here are a tribute to the accuracy of our culture's psychological lore; our recurrent inevitable failures attest to the danger that any explanation may just not appeal to the right facts, may be hollow.

POSTSCRIPT: THREE CONJECTURES ABOUT PSYCHOLOGICAL REALITY

Our capacity to understand and explain human action is, according to the account I have been piecing together, rather like our capacity to communicate with language. It is something we learn to do as we become members of human society, and whose principles we find later very hard to state. Like language it varies from one place and one time to another, and like language there are subtle differences between dialects and idiolects, poised over a suspicion of deep universal similarities. And one is easily led to conjecture that here too the ease with which we master such a marvellous thing and its centrality in our lives results from the presence in human beings of a specific skill of acquiring and using rules, of this variety and this lack of variety, governing the operations of the understanding.[1]

No doubt it is possible to put together into a tighter pattern the pieces of common-sense psychology that I have managed to collect, but it is also evident that there are many pieces left out, and that many of them will have to be found before the connections of even some of the most obvious elements become clear. The extent to which I have been able to piece things together is shown in the Big Picture that decorates this postscript. It is a pretty gappy picture, though. The least misleading way for me to show how the picture might be completed, without pretending to complete it, is to make some grandiose conjectures. They concern the relation between the states of mind attributed to agents in the course of explanations of their actions and the underlying states which might be adduced in an eventual scientific understanding of these actions. The conjectures do not

---

[1] Formulations a little like this are hinted at by Noam Chomsky in the last chapter of *Language and Mind* (Harcourt, Brace, and World, New York, 1968), and in the first chapter of *Reflections on Language* (Pantheon, New York, 1975). One can read the concluding section of Norman Malcolm's *Problems of Mind* (Harper and Row, New York, 1975) as saying something similar.

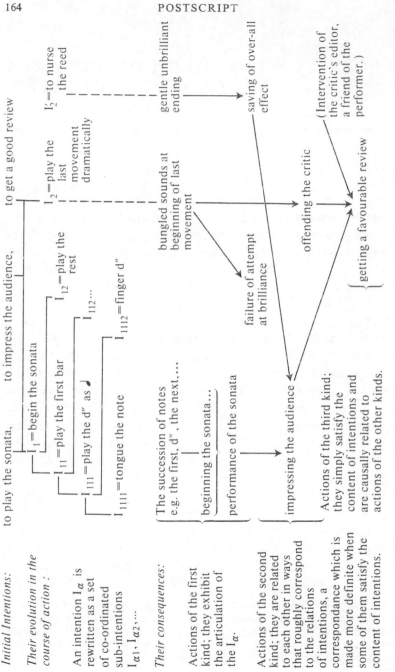

Initial Intentions:

to play the sonata, to impress the audience, to get a good review

Their evolution in the course of action :

An intention I_α is rewritten as a set of co-ordinated sub-intentions $I_{\alpha 1}, I_{\alpha 2}, \ldots$

$I_1 =$ begin the sonata

$I_{11} =$ play the first bar

$I_{111} =$ play the d″ as ♩

$I_{1111} =$ tongue the note

$I_{1112} =$ finger d″

$I_{112} \ldots$

$I_{12} =$ play the rest

$I_2 =$ play the last movement dramatically

$I_2' =$ to nurse the reed

Their consequences:

Actions of the first kind; they exhibit the articulation of the I_α.

Actions of the second kind; they are related to each other in ways that roughly correspond to the relations of intentions, a correspondance which is made more definite when some of them satisfy the content of intentions.

Actions of the third kind; they simply satisfy the content of intentions and are causally related to actions of the other kinds.

The succession of notes e.g. the first, d″, the next, …

beginning the sonata…

performance of the sonata

impressing the audience

bungled sounds at beginning of last movement

failure of attempt at brilliance

gentle unbrilliant ending

saving of over-all effect

offending the critic

(Intervention of the critic's editor, a friend of the performer.)

getting a favourable review

follow from anything I have argued for, but if they were true they would make the ability to handle common-sense psychology the sort of business I believe it to be.

A useful object of comparison is provided by Wittgenstein's attack on the idea that there must be some objective property common to all the people of whom a psychological word is correctly attributed.[2] The conviction that there must be such a common property leads us, he thinks, to postulate a category of particularly gymnastic mental states: images, mental assertions, characteristic feelings, and acts of will, whose function is to provide a unity for all the disparate cases falling under a common mental concept. There's no reason to believe that these things occur where they are postulated to, though, and even if they did occur behind all perceivings and thinkings and actings, they would not actually serve the unifying purpose they are meant to. One thus forces oneself into two deceptions; one tells oneself that there are sensations, mental assertions, and acts of will where there are not, and where there are such things one gives them a causal role they do not have.

Wittgenstein's diagnosis of the situation is that the unity that attributions of a psychological word have does not involve *any* common underlying state of mind. Not that there are not states of mind, ways people are; but what the psychological word picks out is first of all some aspect of the way agents and their actions are related to their environment and embedded in social contexts of co-operation, control, and communication. Moreover, what we direct our application of the words to is not the presence of objective properties and relations, but what needs to be said in these social contexts.

[2] I find the argument easiest to follow in *The Blue and the Brown Books*, see pp. 4–7, 17–20, 143–50. Here I feel that I can almost separate the attack on mental properties from the general 'family resemblance' analysis, which is meant to apply to non-mental properties too. I share the despair of most writers on Wittgenstein's later writings of separating at all clearly this strand of argument from others which get wound around it in the *Philosophical Investigations*. One such inseparable theme there I would express in my terminology first as the claim that one particular 'dialect' of common-sense psychology, which he feels himself surrounded by, makes those who use it particularly subject to myths of subjectivity, and then as attempts to nudge the reader into a less anxious dialect.

The picture this book presents is different. While it is true that episodes of sensing, asserting, and willing do not provide a common fabric for the mental, and true that what about one person at one time makes some psychological term apply need not be what makes the same term apply to someone else, or the same person, on some other occasion, it does not follow that in explaining someone's actions in a common-sense way one is not referring to real causal properties of the person, that a scientific psychology might also appeal to.

As I warned, I am not going to give any very direct or conclusive considerations for this. Instead, here are three grand unsubstantiated claims in the right direction, which are plausible to the extent that they tie together and would explain many particular conclusions in the preceding chapters.

THE UNDERLYING STATES CORRESPOND TO IMPLICIT CONCEPTS OF OUR PSYCHOLOGICAL SCHEMES

The claim admits that in describing a person by use of one's explicit psychological vocabulary one is presenting a mass of information about the agent's situation with respect to the environment and the social context, and that what one says will be directed very often to some particular purpose of communication, expression, instruction, or whatever. These things are done via a very particular procedure and in part directed at a very particular end, though; they match up this complex of situational and social information with the consequences of one or another of the constellation of fundamental nameless states, ways one has learned that people can be, that one's socialization and one's imagination equip one to suppose. The situation is much like that involved in the recognition of spoken words; one hears a confused jumble of sounds, varying from speaker to speaker and from context to context in each person's speech, and one orders and describes these sounds by matching them up against the phonetic possibilities of the language in question, thereby making implicit use of concepts which, unless one is a phonetician, one has no words for.

This pattern was clearest in what I said about belief. There

I tried to describe how the immediate content of an ascription of belief (conjecture, conviction, inclination . . .) varies from occasion to occasion, and how yet there is another content indicated, a latent content as it were, which places the agent with respect to the implicit concepts underlying the category of belief. One manages to express what kind of assertive attitude the agent has to some mental content, and one situates the agent in a referential network. I argued for something similar with respect to desire. The matching-up of implicit concepts with observed behaviour was described in various special cases as a use of a specific kind of imagination in Chapters III and VI. One improvises ways of presenting this inexplicit content, and one fits it to action by a kind of imagination.

I should note that the claim is not that there are particular fixed properties, fixed as part of human nature and part of the nature of any creatures we may be able to treat as psychological beings, which are referred to by the implicit concepts. There is too much evidence that different people do the same things for different reasons, and it is too clear how little constraint psychological common sense places on the workings of the creatures it may be applied to, for that.[3] We are dealing with a scheme rather than a theory. The implicit concepts refer if whenever an explanatory system based on them succeeds in producing explanations it does so because of the applicability to agents of properties and relations which are structured, related to one another, in the way the schematism demands. Whenever one appeals to a belief, for example, there must be a real referential network present, and it must work like a referential network. And though what constitutes a referential network may in different creatures under different circumstances be rather different things there is a definite sense in which as long as the schematism is satisfied there is a unity, a common property to

_____

[3] This is of course a theme of the functionalism of Putnam and Fodor. See Hilary Putnam, 'Minds and Machines', in *Philosophical Papers*, vol. 2 (C.U.P., 1975); J. A. Fodor, *Psychological Explanation* (Harper, New York, 1968). See also David Lewis, 'An Argument for the Identity Theory', in D. M. Rosenthal, ed., *Materialism and the Mind–Body Problem* (Prentice-Hall, Englewood Cliffs, 1971).

all these instances; what you have in each of them is after all reference.

THE PSYCHOLOGICAL AUTONOMY OF
EVERYDAY PSYCHOLOGY

Evidently, if the general drift of what I have been saying is correct, that part of our thinking which is concerned with psychological matters has a certain autonomy. The conceptual autonomy of the psychological was implicit in the programmatic remarks at the end of Chapter I and in the claims of distinctive styles of psychological explanation in Chapters II and V. It might well be that this lack of integration of the psychological into the rest of our thinking, the way we think through matters of motives and beliefs largely independently of non-psychological considerations, is an accident of our culture, a sign of our incorrigible dualism perhaps. My guess is that this is not so, though, and that the autonomy of the psychological is the result of roughly biological constraints on our cognition. We are made to have this department of our thought, it's part of our design, and made so that there are constraints, framings, around the forms it can take.

Too simple forms of this conjecture are clearly false. Our judgements about minds are clearly not just the expression of inherited primate sociality. The truth, I think, is that there is a stratification to psychological thinking, different ends of which are pulled by different forces. At one extreme there is overt use of the psychological vocabulary, which is a thoroughly conceptual business because of its connections with all else that we say and think. And then at the other extreme there is just primate sociality (monkeys, not bishops), limited in its original purposes, and flexible in its new purposes only by virtue of its connections with the other, articulate, end of things.[4]

---

[4] The primal primate is more thinly disguised in some places than others, though. By chance I found myself reading at the same time C. P. Snow's *The Masters* and a *Scientific American* article on social hierarchies in rhesus monkeys. The similarities of motive, of Cambridge in the 1930s and of these somewhat confined and bored creatures, left me for some time in a decidedly socio-biological frame of mind.

It is like the discourse of two people; A is an expert, at getting around in the woods, say, and not much else; B is good at general conversation and calculation. A's vocabulary consists in the concepts of woodmanship, and little else. They function as a team, say to guide strangers through the forest. It is B who speaks to the customers, and so his vocabulary must be wide and flexible enough to handle the questions they are likely to ask and the answers he is likely to give. But he must also talk to A, and he cannot do so in this all-purpose language. B cannot ask A 'how do we paddle as little as possible and still give our clients the impression of having come a long and difficult way, worth a big fee'; A wouldn't understand. He has to ask him about all the routes from p to q, and how long each will take, and so on. And then he has to interpret the answer he gets in terms of his own less-straightforward purposes. B's thought and language has to bridge a conceptual gap; it has to be usable to make contact both with A and with the customers.

A customer listening to B speak will only slowly realize that there are these constraints on the way he answers questions. The more he learns, though, the more his sense of the presence of A and of his powers and limitations will shape his understanding of B. So it is with our understanding of the psychological idiom of our culture. At first we just see the B-part, the generally conceptual and conversational aspect, and then as we understand more and more of it we come more and more to understand, indirectly, via the constraints that are imposed on this B part, its connections with a more fundamental, more expert, less tractable A-part. And of course in so doing we connect the A-faculty in each of us with the B-faculty, and then it is not only harnessed but in some way tamed.

THE CONTINUITY OF COMMON-SENSE PSYCHOLOGY AND SCIENTIFIC PSYCHOLOGY

Philosophers write as if common sense were a body of beliefs, bearing a problematic relation to other bodies of belief, in particular to Science. In everyday idiom common sense is not something people hold but something they have; it is a characteristic of people, closely related to the abilities involved in making practical decisions and foreseeing possibilities. My characterization of common-sense psychology is evidently closer to everyday usage here; I am describing something that is as much a skill as a doctrine. Some can have more of this skill than others; some clearly do. There just are psychologically acute people, just as there are people whose musical, geometrical, or mechanical sensibilities are more live than those of others.

This sensibility naturally gives its possessors an interest in its object, and being obedient citizens of modern culture they naturally wish to be systematic, rigorous, scientific in their pursuit of the object. So we do psychological research in part out of a curiosity in what it is to be human, and we look to the results of this research for help when our psychological acuteness fails to be enough.

This might easily be a mistake, a fraud of our culture.[5] Scientific psychology, aiming at general truths about human nature and human behaviour, *need* not have any continuity with psychological common sense, a skill that aims at truths apt for particular occasions. And the appeal to psychological results in non-academic contexts *is* as often as not a fraud, and one that it is hard to equip people to resist. But the hope is well-founded,

---

[5] This is understating it. In very modern culture psychology has the position that religion once had and philosophy once aspired to. People, real non-academic people, cite the psychologist's authority over the whole range of their lives, and particularly in moral and social matters. Books on how to live one's life are shelved in the psychology sections of bookstores. It is partly in defence against this that we academics, reactionaries all, cling so tightly to our Freudian or behavioural dogmas, which teach above all that psychology is hard and its fruit dry.

Were this a complete mistake, then a very attractive apparent opening out of our culture would be a dead end. The appearance that attracts us is that just as a human capacity for geometrical and combinatorial intuition makes the practice of mathematics possible, and just as physical, mechanical, intuition is harnessed in physical science and is never very far from the experience of the working physicist, so too the capacity to intuit motives and imagine states of mind, which is also just a specific something we humans have, in varying degrees and forms, may be made part of the practice of a science, of something that, supported heuristically by such a capacity, results in solid, experimentally based knowledge. (Think of linguistics.)

I think; it is not simply out of naïvety that we think that this faculty and the intuitions it generates may be harnessed in a science.

What reasons are there for thinking this to be true? They consist essentially in the position of common-sense psychology when seen from the point of view of scientific psychology. The point of view I have been presenting throughout the book and expressing in these conjectures takes common-sense psychology to refer, albeit often indirectly and through the aptness of its explanations as much as through the literal application of its terms, to some of the actual causes of action. I have taken everyday psychological explanations to be *explanations*, and not just satisfying redescriptions of their objects. And moreover the kinds of causes that I have taken everyday psychological explanations to refer to are classifiable in the same way that one would most naturally classify the states that one postulates in cognitive or perceptual psychology. There are broad skills and capacities (Chomsky's Competence), there are improvised means of putting these capacities into action (Chomsky's Performance), and there are transient states of temporary activation of combinations of these. It is hard to see how any scientific psychology of any completeness can fail to include all of these among the causes of behaviour.

Moreover, states from all of these categories are taken in both everyday and most scientific psychology as representational. They are taken to have both referential relations to objects in the world and relations of inference or calculations to each other. J. A. Fodor and S. P. Stich argue that in scientific psychology these two aspects, which are held together in everyday talk of minds by the use of embedded sentences in idioms that ascribe states of mind, are likely to come apart.[6] I do not find this as threatening as it might seem, partly because I do not think they

---

[6] See Fodor's *The Language of Thought*, a series of papers by Stich soon to appear, and my review of Fodor, *Journal of Philosophy* 75, 1978. Arguments more general than those of Fodor and Stich are found in recent work of K. V. Wilkes, which I find, like the others, to underestimate the flexibility of the psychological scheme.

are likely to come completely apart and partly because I think that in everyday psychology too there is a constant tension between the two components of intentionality. This seems to me the issue that is most worth working at if one wants to clarify the possible relations between science and the common-sense idea of the mental.

To say that the states that underlie the application of common-sense psychology are real, that they are a part of the causal net that we hope eventually to be able to trace out, is not to say how large or basic a part of psychological reality they are, for how much of the net they are a basis. It could be that their ultimate importance is quite slight, that on the last analysis they will appear as incidental and rather artificial combinations of the really basic factors. The last analysis is a long way off, though, and on the way to it we seem justified in refining our clumsily practical dialects of common sense and our educable capacities of psychological intuition, so that they may form part of a unified attitude to human nature. How far this may take us is one of the great questions of the age.

INDEX

DATE DUE

12. 15. '81	
4 23. '86	
1. 20. '88	

BRODART, INC.

Cat. No. 23-221